THE NOT SO
GOLDEN
YEARS

THE NOT SO GOLDEN YEARS

Marilyn Fanning

While this book is designed for the reader's personal enjoyment, it is also intended for group study. A Leader's Guide with Victor Multiuse Transparency Masters is available from your local bookstore or from the publisher.

VICTOR

BOOKS a division of SP Publications, Inc.
WHEATON, ILLINOIS 60187

Offices also in
Whitby, Ontario, Canada
Amersham-on-the-Hill, Bucks, England

Recommended Dewey Decimal Classification: 612.67
  Suggested Subject Headings: OLD AGE; MEDICAL CARE FOR THE AGED

Library of Congress Catalog Card Number: 83-51310
ISBN: 0-88207-211-6

Contents

To My Family

My husband, Bill. Our children, Lesley, Claire, and Wayne. Our grandchildren, Christine, Lauren, and Julie; Jason and Christopher; Ivy and Pete.

═Preface═
Waiting for the Total Picture

This book had its beginning in the air. Buckled in an airplane seat, I gazed out the window. Whenever I fly, I feel very close to God, not because He is "up there," but because I know I am totally in His hands. Bible verses came to mind, though I didn't know the chapters and verses. The impact of the words on my mind was so strong that I took a notebook from my purse and wrote them down. Later they formed the basis for most of these chapters.

First I wrote two chapters. I laid them aside for a year. Then I gave them to a friend, a writer, to read. "Do you think you have a book?" she asked.

I laid them aside again. It wasn't until the death of both my parents that I understood God's plan. I had to wait to see the total picture. Waiting is difficult. We see through a glass darkly. As we wait, God's plan unfolds in His way and in His timing.

I pray that this book may be in God's plan and timing for you.

1
A Temporary Resident

"Hear my prayer, O Lord, and give ear to my cry; hold not Your peace at my tears! For I am Your passing guest, a temporary resident, as all my fathers were. O look away from me and spare me, that I may recover cheerfulness and encouraging strength and know gladness before I go and am no more." Psalm 39:12-13, AMP

Nancy's mother was a brilliant business analyst who retired to a condominium in Florida at the age of 65. Suddenly she couldn't write checks or balance her checkbook. A victim of Alzheimer's disease, Nancy's mother is living in a mobile home on her children's property and has a full-time nurse.

* * *

Three times a week Helen visits her 95-year-old mother in a nursing home, taking her treats and the church bulletin, and bringing home her soiled laundry. Helen is unmarried, an only child, age 74.

Henrietta, 58, is a tax specialist with a business office in her home. Every day she gets two grandchildren ready for school, as their parents leave early for work. At noon Henrietta goes to a nursing home to feed her mother lunch.

* * *

Laura is 42, married, and the mother of three teenagers. She and Tom, her husband, take turns each night setting the alarm every two hours to check on Tom's mother, 78, who has had a stroke. A visiting nurse comes daily to bathe her and give her injections.

* * *

From her hospital bed in a nursing home, Eleanor, 71, watched the marriage of her son and his bride. The festivities were held in the day room so that she could attend. "We wanted Mama present, and this was the only way," her son explained.

Turning Our Backs?

A myth has been perpetrated that we are a nation of callous children turning our backs on parents and grandparents, shuffling them off to substandard nursing homes, and abandoning them to strangers. The phrase "putting him (or her) in a nursing home" has become synonymous with caging a sick animal and walking away. Consequently, many adult children become fearful or experience guilt as they face responsibility for a parent who no longer can be self-sufficient.

"It's time to get away from the rhetoric about how awful we are to our elderly," says gerontologist Robert N. Butler, author of the Pulitzer prizewinning book, *Why Survive? Being Old in America.* "The family is the No. 1 caretaker, and is very responsible" ("How America Treats Its Elderly," *Newsweek,* Nov. 1, 1982, p. 60).

Though adult children may want to care for parents at home,

it is not always possible due to a too-small house, employment outside the home, or a divorce. Also, due to the low birth rates of the depression years, there are now fewer adult children to care for the aging.

Under stresses unknown 20 years ago, families are aware of their responsibilities. Help is beginning to come from other sources though slowly. Among them are agencies, either federally funded, staffed by volunteers, or church administered; television specials; books; articles in magazines; health care units; visiting nurses, geriatric day care, and hospice programs. These are providing information or services to help in the care of the aged.

About 90 percent of the respondents to a survey of social service, nursing, and administrative personnel in nursing home facilities reported that elderly persons were admitted to these institutions because relatives or others could not cope with the 24-hour daily stress and demand of administering to their needs. A common response pattern from those surveyed was that at the time of admittance the "family could not take it anymore, they were unable to cope; the situation was threatening the family or marriage."

Nursing home personnel felt that the reluctance and guilt of family members were the main obstacles in trying to meet the needs of stress-related admittances. Yet they felt that a nursing home is still a viable alternative for a family who cannot cope with caring for an elderly person.

"Demographically we have a phenomenon commonly referred to as the 'graying of America,'" said Dr. Noel A. Cazenave, a Temple University sociologist. "In the not so distant future, a large portion of the American population will be 65 or older and we can expect this trend to continue" ("Family Stress Is Fairly Routine," *AARP Bulletin,* September 1982).

Indeed, the Census Bureau projects that the percentage of Americans 65 and over will rise from 11.4 percent in 1981 to 21.7 percent in 2050. According to the Bureau's John Long, "Two things—lower fertility rates and improved life expectancy—will make for a marked change in the relationship of younger people to older people."

Declining birth rates, longer lifespans, and a trend toward early retirement affect the Social Security system. In 1950 births averaged 3.7 children per woman, while today it is only 1.8. Fewer births mean fewer contributors to Social Security and, as a result, more pressure on younger people as they care for the elderly.

Robert Ball, a former Social Security commissioner and now a member of the study panel known as the National Commission on Social Security Reform, described the fundamental difference between the system and all other retirement insurance funds when he wrote that "income from current contributions is used to pay current beneficiaries, rather than being held for retirement of the contributor; thus, the ability to meet future obligations depends on future contributions" ("An In-depth Look at Social Security," *Lynchburg News and Daily Advance*, Nov. 28, 1982).

Flaws in the System

Concern about the future of Social Security, Medicare, Medicaid, and related funds has caused reaction ranging from uneasiness to panic. According to Cyril F. Brickfield, executive director of the American Association of Retired Persons, Medicare is a victim of structural deficiencies in the American health care system. He writes, "Such flaws [in the health care system] have contributed to the soaring inflation that helped push up Medicare expenditures from $5 billion in fiscal 1970 to $22.2 billion in 1981. . . . Ultimately, most authorities believe, soaring Medicare costs will not be reduced without changing the way health care is financed and delivered" ("Competition? It's No Cure-All," *Modern Maturity,* Oct.-Nov., 1982, p. 9).

As medical professors see the average lifespan approaching 85, the need for ways to enhance those later years becomes more evident. Certainly we need more knowledge of the diseases of old people.

In a report to the Senate Special Committee on Aging, Dr. Butler said, "Coming demographic changes constitute the most dramatic trend of the past 100 years in the U.S." To deal with this change, he recommended a high-level policy council, consisting of directors of the National Institute on Aging, the Social Security Administration, and other relevant agencies. "Science has maximized survivorship," observed the former director of the National Institute on Aging, now a pioneer in the Department of Gerontology at Mt. Sinai Medical Center. (Cyril Brickfield, "Time to Gear Up for the Demographic Revolution," *Dynamic Years,* Nov.-Dec. 1982, p. 64).

It is no secret that people are living longer, mainly due to better care and nutrition and research into diseases of the aging. Through Medicaid, Medicare, and veterans' benefits, 63 percent of all federal health dollars go for the care of the elderly. In 1900 the average life expectancy was 49 years; it is now 77 for women and 70 for men. The "older generation" is classified in three groups: *the young old* from 60 to 75; the *middle old* from 75 to 85; and the *old old* who live past 85.

An interesting aspect is that the young old and even the middle old are often coping with the care of the old old. It is important to realize that old people are like young people—they vary in size, mental and physical abilities, emotional needs, drive, and desire for approval. There are no average "over

65s" or "over 85s," anymore than there are average 20-year-olds or 40-year-olds.

The caretaker (or caregiver) of the elderly person is often a woman in her middle years. She may be widowed, needing to work, and perhaps suffering from physical infirmities herself. Sometimes she is also caring for grandchildren while a daughter or son works. The rising divorce rate has increased the need for effective grandparenting at a time when a grandparent is facing not only transitional periods in her own life, but in that of her parents. In other situations, couples have the care of a parent as well as teenagers at home or in college.

All these statistics and real-life scenarios translate into individuals like you and me. Facts, agencies, and research can help in the care of parents, but Christians have access to an even greater Source of wisdom.

We or our parents are not statistics in God's eyes. We are precious to Him. He longs to help us, to guide us in responsible decisions. Even more, our Lord goes through these valleys with us and desires to remove the resentment, guilt, and unforgiveness that beset us. How do we begin?

Asking for Wisdom

In James we read, "If any of you lacks wisdom, let him ask of God, who gives to all men generously and without reproach, and it will be given to him" (1:5). The *Amplified Bible* reads "without reproaching or faultfinding." We may overlook that important phrase when we pray for wisdom in a difficult situation. Sometimes in asking for wisdom, we come to God in anger and with rebellion in our hearts. Ideally, we should confess these sins and *then* request wisdom, but often, in our desperation and need for quick answers, we fail to do this. Yet our wonderful Father hears our pained requests and gives "without reproach or faultfinding."

How we need wisdom in making decisions concerning our parents! We have all read that it is better to keep elderly people in their own homes as long as possible—as long as they can care for themselves adequately. That's a good suggestion (one we'd like made for ourselves), but it is not always easy to know exactly *when* the time for change has come, or *how* to go about it.

More often than not, the "children" see the need for change before the parents. Inability to cook properly or to take the right medication; a fall, illness, or fire; lack of mobility for simple daily tasks such as bathing—all indicate some form of help is needed, though not necessarily a move.

Creative Options

Many people face financial hardship while caring for aged parents. If the parent has a lot of money, more options are available. If there is no money, Medicaid will step in (at least at the time of this writing). When a parent has a small monthly pension and Social Security, for example, it is necessary to decide where the parent will live to the satisfaction (if possible) of all concerned parties. As we pray for the guidance of the Spirit, creative solutions may come to us.

Six brothers and sisters living in different states agreed on an ingenious solution to care for a mother who had no home or money. Each invited Mom to visit for two months at a time. Mom never recognized this conspiracy of love since at the end of each two-month period, one of her children called her and enthusiastically asked, "How about visiting us for a change? We've missed you! Come and spend a couple of months with us."

Happily and obediently, Mom moved on to the home of another child. This way each of the six cared for her two months each year. Success of such an arrangement, however, requires several agreeable siblings, a flexible parent, and suitable accommodations in each home. The point is that through prayer and listening to God, we may indeed receive creative answers to vexing situations.

Another example: Two elderly sisters with varying physical problems chose to live together, sharing expenses, and watching out for one another, rather than each going to live with a child. They have arguments, but these would occur no matter where they lived. Sometimes such an arrangement works for a time, until the dimension of need expands.

Two women who had great difficulty getting along with their own mothers decided to switch! When the aged person lived in the home of a friend, the parent-child friction stopped, and a pleasant boarder-hostess relationship was established. Such a solution may be workable only a short time, or it may last long enough to show all concerned a better way to treat one another.

David's mother needed help but was adamant about giving up her home. David found a student who could live in and prepare the evening meal for herself and David's mother. Again, it was only an interim solution, but one that gave the family time to more fully make arrangements for her future care.

Using some form of home care service may be the answer. Many communities have visiting nurses or nursing assistants who give baths, do light housekeeping, and prepare one meal. A Meals-On-Wheels service is often available. This provides a nutritious main meal for the person who is able to fix only light snacks.

Right Timing
Sometimes a parent is taken into a child's home at the wrong time. The parent may be too young, still well enough to live

alone; or too sick, requiring so much care that an immediate move to a nursing home is required. Change is shock and should be lessened by acting at the right time. As we seek the Holy Spirit's guidance, He shows us the best solution at the right time.

While moving an elderly person to different surroundings is always a traumatic experience, the extent varies with the age and personality of the parent. How we react in old age depends on how we have met stress and change throughout our lives, as well as on physical and chemical changes in our bodies. Suddenly becoming dependent on others for the most basic care is troubling for people at any age, but here we are primarily concerned with the increasing numbers of elderly who need supportive care.

Sociologist Margaret Mead wrote in her last article before her death, "One important change is the enormous increase in longevity. Fifty years ago weak babies died in infancy; adults died of diseases like tuberculosis and diphtheria; the older people who survived were hale and hearty, still able to help, not a burden to their children and grandchildren" ("The American Family: An Endangered Species?" *TV Guide*, Dec. 30, 1978, p. 12).

My father's family is a case in point. A sister died of appendicitis and a brother of tuberculosis. Both were in their 20s. Yet Dad and another sister lived well into their 90s, needing supportive care during the last few years of life.

People of advanced age who are reluctant to leave their homes, either for a home with a relative or for institutional care, sometimes affirm their independence when actually they are dependent on others for transportation, shopping, cleaning, and even cooking.

Aunt Kate, well past 90, washed her dishes from a wheelchair and often could not hear the phone or doorbell. Her "independence" was assured because an only son and daughter-in-law (both in their 60s and holding full-time jobs) did her shopping, laundry, and house maintenance during their lunch hours and weekends. Finally, at age 95, Aunt Kate consented to sell her home and move.

The Effects of Change

After settling a parent in new surroundings, whether in a private home, a retirement home, or a nursing home, the effects of change itself undoubtedly will begin to show on both parent and adult child. Change is shock. If the stay is of long duration, lifestyles, relationships, priorities, and emotions are affected. Aging parents may be as dependent on us as we were on them when we were children. This reversal is shock.

As Christians we begin to ask ourselves, "How much is too much?"/"What does it mean to honor parents?"/ "How do I deal with such emotions as guilt and unforgiveness?" As middle-aged children, we may feel that there are not enough pieces of ourselves to go around to satisfy the needs of a spouse, children, grandchildren, and parents. We may react angrily if we have no time for our own interests.

We serve a Lord who knows and understands all our emotions. We worship a Saviour who came to set us free. Nothing is too hard for God, and we need to please Him first. Having a daily meeting with Him through prayer and Scripture is our first priority.

Because of our faith in God who loves us, who answers prayer, who has promised us wisdom if we ask, we can affirm with Paul, "We are troubled on every side, yet not distressed; we are perplexed, but not in despair; persecuted, but not forsaken; cast down, but not destroyed; always bearing about in the body the dying of the Lord Jesus, that the life also of Jesus might be made manifest in our body" (2 Cor. 4:8-10, KJV).

As I have seen the growing need for parent support and care, I have desired to share my experience as an only child of parents who lived first in their own home, then in our home, their own apartment, and finally, in a nursing home. My prayer is to help other Christians seeking to honor their parents while dealing with transitional patterns in family life. Having no qualifications as psychologist or theologian, I do not pretend to offer expert advice. I share what I have learned during those eight years, and how the grace of a bountiful God met every need.

While counseling a middle-aged woman on the care of her aged mother, a wise doctor observed, "Remember, you can provide for your mother's comfort but not for her happiness." These words contain much truth, even biblical truth. Happiness and the contentment of Christians of any age is dependent on their relationship with Jesus Christ.

2
Let Me Know, Lord

"Lord, make me to know my end, and what is the extent of my days. Let me know how transient I am." Psalm 39:4

Some old people die suddenly, but for most there comes some change, accident, or illness that interrupts the serenity of their lives and propels them into dependence. Often one little episode alters the course of life.

At 82 and 89, my mother and father were independent. Dad still planted large gardens of vegetables and flowers. His fruit trees yielded their crops under his professional hands. Mother canned and made jam, worked needlepoint, and vacuumed her house. Dad did the grocery shopping and all of the driving. Almost every Sunday they were in church. A doctor, who knew them well, saw them regularly, prescribed and counseled according to their needs. Theirs was the kind of life most people in their 80s would like.

Suddenly that one little episode occurred. Mother climbed up on a chair to adjust the hands of her red kitchen clock, lost her balance, fell, and broke an arm. Dad called me, shaken and upset, and urged me to fly to their home in Utica, N.Y. to help.

That particular trip required many decisions. Going then meant leaving my husband, a teenage son, a daughter-in-law and baby who were living with us, and a part-time job. Since there was no other feasible answer, I flew to Utica. Two weeks later, I called Bill.

"Do you think we could manage if I brought Mother and Dad back with me? Her arm is in a sling and she's helpless."

"Where would we put them—with the kids here, and the baby?" Bill questioned. Then he suggested, "I suppose they could use our room—we could sleep on the den sofa bed."

It was settled. I flew back with Mother, but since Dad adamantly refused to "get his feet off the ground" Bill drove the 600 miles north to bring him back by car.

How Mother enjoyed her trip! Even with her injured arm, she approached her first flight in a spirit of gaiety and adventure. "I've always wanted to fly!" she affirmed happily.

Four months passed before they returned to their home in Utica, ending a period with four generations living under one small roof, each representing different schedules, attitudes, and dispositions. The Lord did some refining work on Bill and me, molding and shaping us as we asked for His guidance.

Suggesting a Move
Soon after their return home, we suggested that they consider moving into an apartment in Lynchburg, Va. near us, but they didn't heed our advice. I wrote them and phoned them, outlining the advantages. Relatives called me long distance to protest: "We can't take care of your parents—we're too old ourselves! It's up to you to do something!"

Bill and I prayed every day that God would show my parents the right thing to do. After six months Mother called to tell us they had put their house on the market. Six months from the day of that call, the house sold. I made several plane trips to try to sort, sell, discard, and pack. I say *try* because neither Dad nor Mother wanted to discard a thing—not a nail or necklace, chair or carton, rug or rag. The house and basement were crammed with precious possessions and dusty antiques, as well as worthless accumulations. My parents seemed unable (or unwilling) to distinguish between them; they opposed any suggestions. For several years my aunts and I had encouraged my parents to clean out. Magnificent treasures of our colonial past mingled with stacks of egg cartons and bent nails; heavily varnished old chests lined the basement walls and were crammed with jars, linens, papers, and tools. Towering armoires displayed shelves of florist ribbons, business records, and vases—all from the years when "E. T. Hermant and Son" was a thriving floral vendor. Valuable tools mixed with dried-up paint cans. Mountains of magazines lined the garage and outbuilding, producing a fire hazard.

"He keeps everything!" my mother snorted, shaking her head at my father.

"Ha, ha, ha!" Dad emphasized his retaliation loudly. "*Me?* How about those bolts of material you bought in 1950? I never saw you make dresses out of 'em!"

"Material, huh!" Mother's nose went up in the air. "Let's discuss what you plan to do with 18,000 clay pots!"

"I plan," Dad replied deliberately, "to *use* them!"

It was only one of hundreds of heated exchanges that grew louder and more frequent through the years. Somehow they needed these arguments to infuse life into their relationship.

Mother's best pretense at cleaning out occurred whenever

we visited them in Utica. Cornering me in her bedroom, she steered me toward one of her dressers and suggested, "Let's look at these things and you tell me what to do with them."

The first time this occurred I was eager and pleased as we carried each drawer, groaning under its weight, and placed it in the middle of the bed. Several hours later, we carried each drawer back just as full, cartons and wastebaskets still yawning at our feet.

While staying with Mother at her home following a hospitalization, we tried again. "What's the use?" I asked angrily. "You're never going to throw out or give anything away!"

Mother was angry too. "You have no sentiment. You don't care how important these things are to me."

The Beginnings of Guilt

It was the beginning of a long-term battle over the next few years. Frustrated and guilty, I realized that even though I was a grandmother myself, I still desired the approval of my mother; I did not want to hurt or disappoint her. The first real naggings of guilt began to appear—guilt that Jesus would one day remove.

At Christmastime Mother phoned, begging me to come up as she "just couldn't deal with anything." My husband refused to let me fly to Utica during the holidays, saying I must not leave him, our children, and grandchildren. Nor did I want to. This was one of the many times I recognized self-centered attitudes so often a result of the aging process.

Meanwhile, I had searched for the right apartment in Lynchburg, one that would accommodate their furniture and mode of living. The one I selected seemed perfect. It was on the first floor, but the balcony faced the yard on a second-floor level. I sent them photos of the complex, as well as a floor plan. The rooms were spacious, and it was only a five-minute drive from our house. For the next year and a half, Mother and Dad adjusted to their new place, making friends with residents of other apartments, getting their own meals, and watching television together. It was good for me to have them close, knowing I would be quickly available in the event of an emergency.

That emergency came on Father's Day, 1975. I was about to leave to pick them up for dinner when I received a phone call from Mother. Her voice was pitched higher and louder than usual. "Dad has fallen—and he can't get up!"

"I'll be right there," I assured Mother. Though the drive took only minutes, my shoulders tensed painfully as I sped past houses and trees. During that short mile and a half, I thanked God for His presence and His care. How blessed we are not to know the future, I have thought many times since that day. Hundreds of trips—to the emergency room, to the hospital, to the nursing home were yet to come. I did not know that, of course.

"Why Father's Day?" I asked aloud. I remembered another Father's Day in 1958 when my husband, still shaking, opened the kitchen door to tell me and our three small children, "I've run over our new puppy!"

Amid sobs and tears, Bill hurriedly carried the limp body to bury it in the backyard. I recalled with wonder how our oldest daughter, just 11, quieted us all with the words, "We must stop crying! Think how hard this is for Daddy on Father's Day!"

Jolted back to the present, I ran up steps and used my key to open the apartment door. I rushed to the bedroom where Dad lay on the floor. He had slipped while bending over to pick up a pencil, and lay on his back, totally helpless and in pain. Because Mother had been asleep in her lounge on the balcony with the door closed, she had not heard his cries for help for at least a half hour. "I waited till I heard her slide open the door," he groaned. "And then I called as loud as I could." Even with her hearing aid, Mother's deafness caused many communication difficulties.

Dealing with Emergency

Now she was depending on me to do something. I knelt beside Dad and questioned him while covering him with a blanket. Taking his hand, I prayed aloud, which caused Mother to leave the room in tears. To my surprise, Dad also prayed aloud, and in great faith. "Help me, Lord! You are my Redeemer! I pray You'll help me now!" Other than offering a blessing on Thanksgiving, I never heard my father pray aloud in all his 91 years. Helplessness was foreign to this man of sturdy German and French parents. Usually independent, Dad could repair clocks, cook a scrumptious breakfast, and give himself daily insulin injections.

At that moment of emergency, I did not ask myself if this independence had ended, for my father had extraordinary recuperative power and was seldom ill, except for the chronic condition of diabetes. He was careful about his diet, counting and recording calories in a little black book he kept on the kitchen table. He exercised his arms and legs for minor arthritis, kept records of his finances, and wrote his own checks. His lifelong volatile temper had not improved; I seldom spoke to him if he was at his desk, for his bookkeeping had become an increasingly difficult chore, and he hated interruption.

It didn't take long to decide who to call for help. At that time our son was an emergency medical technician. A young father, compassionate, and capable, he arrived quickly and examined Dad. Hearing a roar of pain, he looked up frowning. "His hip is definitely broken."

Two days passed before the hip could be repaired. While he was in the operating room, Mother, age 84, sat stiffly, patting his hospital bed. I stood by the window, watching birds dip their wings as they avoided a protruding hospital column. Suddenly I smelled antiseptic and heard the door of Dad's room open wide. Wearing rumpled green, Dr. Miller whisked off his cap and smiled at Mother and me.

"Some break!" he exclaimed. "In four places. We've put in pins." Shaking his head, he marveled, "Ninety-one years old with muscle like a man of 40. Amazing."

Dad was indeed an amazing man. Though born in the days of the one-room schoolhouse (I still have the slate he used), and with only a ninth-grade education, he had an engineering mind, inventive and discerning. His humorous poetry expressed a grasp of the world's future problems long before the words *additives* and *pollution* were everyday language. Part of a lengthy poem composed in 1935 reads:

> In these days of indigestion
> It is oftentimes a question
> As to what to eat and what to leave alone.
> For each microbe and bacillus
> Has a different way to kill us
> And in time they always claim us for their own.
>
> There are germs of every kind
> In every food that you can find
> In the market or upon the bill of fare.
> Drinking water's just as risky
> As the so-called deadly whiskey,
> And it's often a mistake to breathe the air.

As a lifelong florist, (a vocation thrust upon him by family pressure), my father did more than grow, plant, and sell flowers. He climbed ladders and stairs, coaled boilers, repaired trucks, chopped wood, hammered, and hauled. No wonder his muscles were strong!

Dealing with Dad

That night after surgery, however, his strength became a deterrent to rest—both his and mine. Dad's age and diabetes limited the choice of medication; delusion, hallucination, violence, and terror were his bedmates. Weeping, I tried to control him as he tore at the tubes in his sutures.

"Please," he whined, "get this contraption off my leg!" His blue eyes penetrated as he accused me of harassing him. "How can a daughter treat her father this way?"

I called for the nurse, who informed me that he could not have a sedative; however, she could hire an aide to relieve me for the rest of the night. Gratefully I accepted. Returning home at 2 A.M., I sank exhausted into bed.

Because of my father's extraordinary health and vitality, I refused to believe that grit and physical therapy would not restore him to independence again, regardless of age. As I left the hospital one day, I met a minister friend at the front door. The perfume of blooming bushes, the penetrating warmth of a June sun, and my natural optimism lifted my spirit—until my friend asked about Dad.

"He's doing great. Cleans everything on his hospital tray. And they took him to therapy again today."

"What will you do next?" Bob asked. "Have you looked at nursing homes?" For a moment I couldn't answer. "Why, I expect he'll do well enough to get back to his cane, and go home," I said.

"He'll never be up and around again. Not at his age. This takes too much out of 'em. See you later." He ambled across the street as I stood there, with weak knees and a tightening in my chest. The perfume and sun were gone. In my heart I knew he was right. I had watched Dad in therapy as he perspired, his arthritic hands gripping the bars, his face contorted in pain. I knew another move was coming.

Preparing for the Next Move

I prayed what I call my "prepare prayer." So often I have asked God to prepare the way, prepare the heart, prepare me. Several definitions of *prepare* are to "make ready" and "to make receptive." As I turned to the Lord for the next step, I asked Him to do just that—to prepare the place, and to prepare the hearts of Dad—and Mother—to accept the next move.

In looking for the right nursing home for a parent, choices can be limited, as mine were, by availability. If the needs of a parent are primarily for skilled care, investigate this type of provision. Perhaps, however, a parent cannot be kept at home for other reasons than physical incapacitation. In that case, facilities for companionship and recreation, as well as nursing care, are of paramount concern. Finances usually are a major factor. Dad's immediate needs were for nursing care and physical therapy, and I considered the proximity of the center too, for my convenience.

When he was moved by ambulance to his new space—half a room—I thought of his background. He had lived most of his life in the same area, witnessed the moving of New York's Mohawk River and the installation of the Barge Canal. He had delivered flowers by horse and buggy, sometimes driving through ice and water. His spacious property housed tractors and tools, barns, trucks, and greenhouses. He now had two drawers, some

clothes and slippers, a few books, and a razor. How we need to
know that for most of us life shrinks; only our relationship with
Christ expands, *if we choose that early in life.*

The reality of birth, life, and death pressed on me as I settled
my father in his room, soothing, answering him, and loving him.
I did love this lusty, loud, and sometimes irritable old man. I had
been born when he was 42, his only child. He had wanted a boy,
but I never felt I was supposed to be a boy, nor did my father
reject me. In fact, late in life, over and over he told me: "What
would we do without our daughter!"

Life was never the same again after the day he bent over to
pick up a pencil and fell. This once-robust man plodded forward
with a walker, painfully, haltingly; the body and mind that had
functioned smoothly, even brilliantly, gradually deteriorated,
expressing signs of helplessness and senility.

"And now my soul is poured out within me; days of affliction
have seized me" (Job 30:16).

I, his only child, watched, prayed, and learned; meanwhile,
caring also for a mother whose strength gradually failed.

Another Move

Soon after Dad entered the nursing home, the doctor advised
us that Mother could not manage alone in her apartment, which
confirmed my observation. She frequently had dizzy spells when
she got out of bed at night to go to the bathroom, or when she
turned too quickly. Suppose, alone in her apartment, she fell
and lay there for hours? I thought of how long Dad had lain
helpless before Mother heard his cries.

Sometimes food burned and the kitchen exuded smoke
while Mom napped in her bedroom. At these times Dad's keen
sense of smell had rescued them. But now who would check on
Mother?

"I'll never come to live with my daughter!" I heard my mother say when she was younger, but life has a way of changing those decisions for us. With the expense of Dad in the nursing home, we could not stretch the income to meet costs of an apartment and round-the-clock help (even if available). Once again my husband and son moved the furniture, this time into our basement.

3
The Things of Others

"Look not every man on his own things, but every man also on the things of others." Philippians 2:4, KJV

Charles was rubbing Dad's scalp with a flourish one day as Mother and I arrived at Dad's room. He did it with an air of professionalism, whisking the towel into the air and capping the bottle of antiseptic noisily. "This is very good for dandruff," he affirmed.

Mother had not yet noticed what he was doing. Holding on to the foot of the bed, she eased herself into the chair. Failing eyesight and hearing, as well as lack of concentration, usually combined to make her oblivious to her surroundings. Dealing with this aspect of old age was very difficult for me.

"Well, how are you, Daddy?" Mother asked her husband. She had missed the dandruff routine.

While they chatted, Dad in his wheelchair, and Mother leaning forward to hear him better, I turned to Charles. He was a tall, thin man about 40, one of the orderlies in the nursing home. Six men were his charges, and he was responsible for all their personal care. This included baths, making beds, cleaning up after accidents, giving enemas, and supervising meals. Charles had a gift for his job—a desire to please and a natural ability to communicate with elderly men. He knew when to baby them, and when to be stern. Giving the scalp treatment was an example of his "going the second mile" for those in his care.

Smiling, I said, "Charles, I really appreciate your care of Dad. There aren't many like you."

He raised his eyebrows just a bit, indicating his thanks. "Well, the Listerine is almost gone. You might want to buy a bottle. It's cheaper than if they buy it for you."

"All right. Say, it looks to me like your ankle is swollen."

"I twisted it, and it sure is sore. Well, I must see if Mr. Elton has finished his lunch." In a limp and a flash he was gone.

Imagine my astonishment when I learned the next week that Charles had been fired.

"He's an alcoholic," the nurse told me, "and it's such a shame."

"A shame!" I cried out. "He's the best orderly here. He has taken such good care of Dad, and Dad really likes him. Couldn't you keep him anyway?"

She shook her head. "It's been going on a long time. He doesn't show up some days—doesn't even call. We can't depend on him. He was given three warnings. Then yesterday he came in to work drunk."

Showing Interest in the Staff

When a parent becomes a resident of a nursing facility, family members relinquish some responsibility. To insure proper care of a loved one, however, it is necessary to know the staff. Paul instructs, "Look not on your own things, but also on the things of others"—the interests and concerns of others. In this case we must not only bear the burdens of caring for parents' needs, but of understanding the problems of the staff who serve our loved ones.

Eileen, a middle-aged aide who had been on staff for three years, went home after a 7 to 3 work shift to nurse her own mother. Joe, another orderly, went to school full time, and worked the eight-hour night shift. Alice was a capable charge nurse whose husband was dying of cancer and whose son lay unconscious after a fall at a construction site.

As I visited my father day after day, week after week, bringing my mother with me, I felt compassion for these people who worked under difficult personal circumstances. How often I heard visitors complain, expecting far more of these "servants" than they themselves would be willing to give. Showing interest in these workers builds a rapport which often results in an opportunity to share Christ. Encouraging them to give the best of themselves to their jobs and offering words of appreciation at the right time, is beneficial to them and to those they care for.

Though I no longer worked as a broadcaster and writer at a local television and radio station, I continued to write at home. A Christian magazine published my four-generation household story, and Dad had a copy at his bedside. One by one the aides and nurses read the article, which resulted in several opportunities to share the joy of the Lord. A few confided their current heartaches and asked for prayer.

Dorothy, an aide in her mid-30s, suffered from anemia. She was tiny too, and I often wondered how she lifted some of the patients. One day, noticing her ashen face and eyes dark with fatigue, I asked her if she felt all right. She replied that she did not and that she was waiting for results of her latest blood test. She was a Christian and had shared with me her mother-in-law's recent death and brief glimpse of heaven's beauty as she died. Dorothy had been with her. "I loved her very much," she told me. "She was only 52, but I know where she is."

Dorothy's kindness spilled over in the care of her patients. I watched her gentleness as she coaxed one old lady to eat her lunch, calling her Sugar and encouraging her, patiently spooning food into her mouth.

Then one day I saw Dorothy in the lobby, painfully propped in a chair waiting for her ride home. She had helped an orderly prevent an old man from falling to the floor, and as the patient resisted her, she had injured her own back severely. She was never able to return to work.

Dealing with the Difficult

Not all the aides or orderlies are kind and loving; not all make good decisions, nor do they know how to treat their charges. I am thinking of John whose every move and gesture signaled rebellion in his job. A student at a Christian college, he worked part time and evidently hated every minute of it. Many aides simply take the job because it's a way to earn money. For a few weeks John was Dad's orderly, snapping the sheets as he made the bed, angrily pushing the wheelchair. He rarely spoke to Mother when she visited Dad with me. One day all his resentment burst forth.

"Come to the shower room with me!" he demanded. "I can't do anything to please him!"

Dad's disposition was less than pleasant, and at this time, and in this place, and at his age, it had not improved. However, I had grown used to him, knowing what should or should not be said. John had neither the time nor the inclination to try.

I followed John as he pushed Dad's wheelchair to the men's shower room. Breathlessly I ran to keep up. Settled on the shower chair, naked and shivering, Dad fussed and winced in pain. John indicated the faucets and the temperature gauge. "He complains it's either too hot or it's too cold! Watch!" John was shouting above the rush of the water.

"OOOOh! That's cold!" yelled Dad, as if on cue. As John changed the flow, Dad hollered that it was too hot. I let the water run on my wrist. It felt pleasantly warm.

"John, I think it's OK. Look. You have a temperature gauge. Why don't you go by that and the feel of it yourself? Just do your job the best you can."

"Well, he hauled off and hit me one day," John said, gritting his teeth.

I had no doubt that he had. As Dad progressed—or regressed—into senility, his physical strength increased, and sometimes he fought wildly—hitting, kicking, yelling. The worst was ahead, but I left John to complete his job of showering my father.

I was not surprised one day to find that John was no longer there.

The importance of caring helpers is illustrated in a letter we received from Elsie, the daughter-in-law of Bill's Aunt Kate. Aunt Kate (Nana) had finally adjusted to her surroundings at age 95 and Elsie wrote:

> Nana stays about the same and doesn't complain anymore—in fact she tells us how nice everyone is to her and that the food is good.
>
> Now our troubles have started with my mom and dad. As you know, Dad has had two strokes and is becoming more and more of a care. He is very demanding and is now up about every two hours all night long. He is pretty good

in the daytime—watching television and smoking his cigars. He eats beautifully and never complains, but the evenings and nights are becoming worse and worse.

Mother was taken to the hospital suddenly about a month ago because of bleeding. They took all kinds of tests and finally removed a polyp from her stomach. They did this down through the throat so there was no surgery required; however, she is very weak and run down. The doctor finally said she could no longer take care of Dad.

I had to stay with him around the clock for about a week and a half and then I was able to get two sisters to stay with him on a 24-hour basis for $100 a day. They were in their 40s and had to alternate every two days because he called for one thing or another so often. I think the week and a half that I stayed with him took 10 years off my life. I don't know how my mother stood it as long as she did.

Anyway, Dad is now in a private rest home. He is really getting more care than in the place where Nana is and that is supposed to be the best in the area. I don't know how long they will keep Dad because it is not a health-related or a skilled nursing home, but they have very kind, caring aides who are taking care of him beautifully. It's so much more like home than the bigger places.

Mother stayed with me for about a week when she came home from the hospital and then I had her out for dinner every night for another week. Now she is home and just needs to get her strength back. I hope she doesn't insist on keeping that big house because it's just too much work for her, and Bob cannot take care of two places.

Martha's situation was stressful too. Her mother was kept at home in a lovely apartment, but required round-the-clock aid. This meant that Martha was responsible for hiring and firing any number of nurses, sitters, or aides. The interpersonal difficulties were enormous. Not only did we pray for nurses for Martha, but we asked God to give her discernment about the problems between her mother and the helpers. Sometimes helpers are jealous of one another; sometimes it is difficult to know whether the aide is really incompetent, or if the patient is imagining things which are not true. Such situations are not only trying, they cause anger and stress in both parent and adult child.

Bearing One Another's Burdens

To look upon the interests of others—to bear one another's burdens—the Word is clear on these points (Gal. 6:2). One day at the nursing home, Paul, a friend whose mother-in-law was also a patient, discovered a thoughtless change made in the living habits of a blind patient. She had been moved to another room, and since she was in the bed near the window instead of the one near the door, she was unable to move about in her darkness without stumbling. Paul found her one day groping for a familiar night table which, because of the reverse furniture arrangement, was located now on the other side of the bed. This patient had no family; a bank conducted her affairs. Paul advised the charge nurse that little Miss Whiting should be returned, if not to the same room, at least to the familiar side of the room, where she could feel her way around in confidence. The administration obliged and Miss Whiting again became oriented to the familiar surroundings. In addition, Paul took the time to hold her hand and pray with her and explain what had happened. Before that, little Miss Whiting had no one to be her advocate.

Suggestions for Visitors

If we are regular visitors to nursing homes, we need to pray that we may be the helpers God desires—knowing when to become involved and to what extent.

In order to bring balance and common sense into our visits with a parent or friend in a nursing home, we need to be alert to specific ways of sharing, listening, and just being there that relieve the distress and anxiety experienced by those in the home and those who visit. Not all of the following suggestions apply to every patient; each is in a different state of health and possesses varying abilities of comprehension and enjoyment. In addition, it is good to check with the charge nurses before bringing food, flowers, or other items that might be inappropriate for health reasons.

• *Share food.* Most patients eat meals alone. Bring two glasses and a milkshake; divide a favorite dessert; cut a piece of fruit and eat it with a loved one. Eating *with* the patient lets him know that we enjoy his company and encourages eating. Sometimes a treat left on a bedside table is unnoticed or forgotten if nursing aides do not help the person eat it later.

Occasionally, order a hospital tray and share a full meal together. This is a way to learn firsthand the quality of the food served, and an opportunity to observe the ability of the person to feed himself, as well as to enjoy fellowship.

• *Share reading material.* Perhaps a parent can no longer hold reading materials or see well enough to read. We can read a passage from Scripture, or from the church newsletter or daily newspaper. If we sense the person's mind has wandered, we can repeat the reading. Often attention spans are brief. Touching may help reinforce awareness as we read.

We can recall past activities together, even if they weren't ours, by bringing an illustrated magazine that expresses a parent's former hobbies or interests.

Sometimes correspondence addressed to the patient is left on the table or in a drawer and may be unopened. We can read it aloud slowly. If the parent is able to write, encourage signing seasonal greeting cards to friends and relatives. We can address the envelopes.

• *Share beauty.* Bring one lovely flower in a vase and tell where it came from—garden, a friend, or a florist shop. When bringing or sending a greeting card, choose one with bright colors and bold print. Gold lettering and pastels do not impress dim eyes. Colored snapshots of children, grandchildren, and pets; calendars with bright scenes; small crafts—all express love and cheer. Better yet, bring grandchildren or great-grand-children in person. Most nursing homes allow them to visit. Outgoing youngsters will climb on laps with smiles and hugs; shy ones learn about caring through such visits.

Sharing beauty may also be a pleasant pastime in the warmer months if the patient can go outdoors with help or in a wheel-chair. Small things we take for granted often please aged peo-ple: the rustle of leaves, the songs of birds, visitors and employees coming and going through the front door. My father admired the different models of cars pulling up to the door, while Mother scrutinized the changing fashions and hairdos. Involvement wards off apathy and depression.

When programs and performers are brought to the home for the patients' enjoyment, try to attend occasionally. Recreation-al activities have a lot to do with the mental health of the patient who is able to share, watch, or participate. Complimenting the director of recreation, offering to assist occasionally, particular-ly at holiday functions, and attending once in a while, combine to encourage programs at these facilities. We should also en-courage the parent to attend or participate if he is able.

• *Stay awhile.* This is not always convenient, especially when we have other family members at home to care for, or a full-time job outside the home. Usually it is more important to visit less often and stay longer, unless the loved one is extremely ill and it is necessary to visit daily to encourage the patient.

Sitting by the chair or bedside is an opportunity to catch up on some of our neglected chores, such as mending or opening mail, writing a letter, or making a grocery list. Watching TV together is another possibility, if there's a set in the room. When a parent has been hospitalized for a long time, constant personal attention is not necessary. Our relaxed presence, even though we are doing something, relates our caring. Sometimes such a period of quiet encourages the patient to share thoughts, fears, or questions that he or she might not otherwise bring up during a brief stay.

• *Listen.* This can be discouraging, especially when parents or friends can no longer communicate meaningfully. Minds wander, they hallucinate, and recall incorrectly. It is important to keep our own minds and hearts on Jesus during these difficult times. We can't dismiss a parent's anxiety with simple cheer; rather we must take complaints seriously and check with those in charge. Ask the Lord for His wisdom and guidance. A parent's peace of mind often depends on reassurance.

The Christian life is one of relationships. Balance is needed as we learn to express ourselves to others, to listen with our hearts as well as our ears, and to take the actions we understand to be right. There is a tension between our actions and our obedience to God's Word and His will. He is gracious to hear us and to instruct us as we tune in.

4
Not As We See

"For God sees not as man sees, for man looks at the outward appearance, but the Lord looks at the heart." 1 Samuel 16:7

"Well, the Lord knows my heart."

Have you heard people say that to cover up a tactless remark or questionable action? Perhaps you have said it. I have, and in a self-righteous manner that I know grieved my Lord. We think that we can excuse ourselves because we believe that deep inside we have a right motive. We think we know our hearts, but in Jeremiah we read, "The heart is more deceitful than all else and is desperately sick; Who can understand it? I, the Lord, search the heart, I test the mind" (17:9-10). In all of us (even in those with so-called low self-esteem) there exists a level of ego that says what I feel inside is what is important. There is, however, a sphere of thought and motive that is known only to the Lord. We need to ask Him if that sphere is pleasing to Him.

Considering relationships with our parents will be more fruitful if we first assess our relationships with God. We must ask, "Is Jesus Christ Lord of my life?" When we want God's will above ours in every situation, we have made Him Lord. *Want* is the key, for then God can show us, can guide us through His Word, through circumstances, and friends, through quiet communion with Him. During the midyears of our lives, no greater blessing is ours than to know the Saviour in such a way. Then we can share Him with our aged parents, and can teach our children and grandchildren the serenity that comes from Him. "The weak need My strength. The strong need My tenderness. The tempted and fallen need My salvation. The righteous need My pity for sinners. The lonely need a Friend. The fighters need a Leader" (A.J. Russell, Ed., *God Calling*, Spire Books, p. 100).

Let us pray, "Lord, show me now where I really am in my relationship with You. Help me to be truthful to You and to myself. I desire to please You and to be free from guilt, resentment, depression, and fear. I know and affirm that these do not belong in my life if I am to serve You and others."

Where Are *You*?

_____I believe in God and I pray now and then.

_____I believe in God and go to church but I don't have a personal relationship with Jesus.

_____I believe in God and know Jesus died for my sins, but I am too busy and tired to think about it or to pray.

_____I accepted Jesus as my Saviour when I was young, but I seem to be living my life alone now and trusting in my own strength and abilities.

_____I read the Bible, but it doesn't have real meaning in my life.

_____I was raised in a Christian home and apply these princi-
ples to my life. I try hard.

_____I have too much resentment and guilt in my life to think
that God would ever forgive me or care about me.

_____I am so angry with God for all the trials and tragedies in
my life that I can't pray or read the Bible.

_____(Fill in the way you feel)

No matter which appraisal you checked, there is hope. Jesus
came to give abundant life (John 10:10) and He is able. You may
begin a new life with Him right now, receiving forgiveness and
the gift of the Holy Spirit. God knows what is in your heart, but
He wants you to acknowledge your feelings to Him. Tell Him
you are willing to unburden yourself and cast your cares on
Him.

We need to spend time with Him as we do with a loved one;
to know He forgives; to know that trials come to us for a
purpose (Rom. 8:28). As we deal with crises and trials, having
a flexible personality carries us through. Being so in tune with
God as to perceive His timing in situations is learned and comes
from spending time with Him. While we jog, drive to work,
vacuum, take a shower, or wait in a doctor's office, we can
effectively meditate on a verse and ask for His wisdom. His
Word is stored in our hearts, to be released in times of need.
There is no substitute for this, whether we are saints of many
years or new Christians.

Caring for Mother

For a year and one-half Mother lived with us while Dad was in
the nursing home. This meant that three times a week I drove
Mother to see Dad. Preparing for the visit took a great deal of
time, for Mother moved slowly. Bathing, dressing, eating—all

took longer. As I tried to clean house, wash, and prepare meals, she would call frequently. The faucet wouldn't work, her earring dropped, her pocketbook disappeared.

One snowy day as we returned from our visit with Dad, my small car stubbornly wedged its wheels in the snow at the end of our long winding driveway. Had I been alone, I could have abandoned it there and walked to the house, but Mother couldn't walk. I called Bill at work and he arrived in 20 minutes, but was unable to move the car. Mother, shivering, began to chuckle. She thought it an adventure! Imagine her delight when her ingenious son-in-law assisted her into a metal lawn chair, and pushed her, sleigh-fashion, up the long driveway to the door! During the next few years, Mother forgot the names of her grandchildren, whether or not the doctor had visited, and what she had for lunch, but she never forgot her winter adventure!

Soon after this winterlude, Mother failed rapidly. Her cataracts had progressed to the point where every room was too dark, or too light for her. She needed regular assistance in the bathroom and with bathing. Dinnertime was a struggle. What should have been a pleasant time (Mother loved to eat) became a tense time. Unwilling to adjust to our schedule, she insisted on hers. Though we got up at 6 o'clock, Mother slept till 9 (when she expected a substantial breakfast). She liked to listen to nightly television till 11:30, with the volume so loud we could not sleep. When we requested that she turn it off, she became angry and pouted. During this time her physical needs increased and in lifting and helping her I injured my back.

The mother now struggling to navigate a walker had playfully chased me with a raw fish many years ago. Her voice, now slurred and sometimes raspy, had yodeled like an Alpine climber and sung hymns in harmony. Hands that once could knit and crochet, couldn't button a sweater.

Missing the Best

Something was gone—a *joie de vivre,* an energy that was exclusively hers. I was her only crutch, a link with the past. Somehow at this period we missed the best in one another; we were not free enough to be fully honest. Though we shared in prayer and she asked me questions about the Bible; though in earlier days we went together to Christian Women's Club and Women's Aglow meetings, somehow the difference of generations was markedly present in our relationship. Our interests were totally different. The most sewing I did was to replace a button or suffer through a hem, while Mother executed Swedish darning and intricate needlepoint. The most reading she did was an occasional magazine, while in earlier years I read every book in our bookcase. Mother put off letter-writing indefinitely; I wrote stories from the age of seven.

I know now that Mother's demands for attention were a replacement for occupations of the past; my neurotic attention to those demands was my way of renewing a childhood obedience, no longer appropriate for a woman in her 50s.

What really caused me great concern was the effect all of this had on my husband. He had been hospitalized a number of times for heart and pulmonary problems, and I observed the strain of Mother's demands on him. One morning, after a particularly difficult day for all of us, including a visit to see Dad, I "took my prayer station." Sitting on a sofa that faced a large window, I opened my Bible and read, "I will stand on my guard post and station myself on the rampart; and I will keep watch to see what He will speak to me, and how I may reply when I am reproved" (Hab. 2:1).

I needed reproving. I felt angry with my mother, trapped by her demands. Bill and I had so little time to talk or share alone; and if Mother turned on her television, it was so loud, our conversation competed with the screeching wheels of a TV show. Asking her to close the door offended her. Yes, I felt trapped between pleasing a mother as a little girl should, and being the wife God intended me to be.

As I sat before Him that morning, I asked Him to help me, to show me His answer. Once an energetic, well-balanced woman, I had become shaky, lame, tense, irritated. "Father, forgive me," I prayed. "I am afraid for Bill. I acknowledge before You that I fear for his health. I want wholeness for all of us."

God knew my heart. He knew I had thought about Mother being with Dad in the same nursing home. She needed help now; I had no time for anything but her care. Of course the Lord knew my heart. When friends said, "Oh, it's so hard for you— your mother with you and your father to visit too!" I felt fleshly self-pity rising like a fresh batch of dough. They saw the outward appearance, but the Lord saw self-pity, resentment, anger, rebellion. There was nothing to hide from Him that day as I sat before Him.

Seeking an Answer

Then peace began to flow through my body, "peace like a river." I seemed to hear the question, "Who is first? Your husband or your mother?" I dialogued with God: "Lord, I really want Mother in the room with Dad. Then I could visit them together, and Mother would be with her husband, and I with mine. I thank You that they have money, and I trust You to give me the right answer. Free me from self-pity, fill me with Your Spirit and Your wisdom."

I sat a little longer. It was 8 A.M. No sound came from Mother's room. Then I prayed a way I had not prayed before. I "put out a fleece" (Judges 6:36-40). I knew this wasn't a good way to pray on a regular basis, but I felt led to do this. "Father," I whispered, "if this is Your will, let there be a room available when I call the nursing home." At 9 o'clock I phoned and talked to the administrator. No, there wasn't a room available. As I hung up, I was disappointed, yet I knew from the peace in my heart that God was faithful. I could trust Him. Mother was not yet awake—I usually had to call her several times while preparing her breakfast. As I set a place for her at the table, the phone rang. It was 9:15.

"Mrs. Fanning?" It was the administrator at the home. "I was mistaken. The man in the room with your father has just been checked out, and the bed in his room is available for your mother."

My prayer had been answered, even to the exact room; but I had yet to face Mother with this new arrangement!

Executing the Answer

A big red pickup parked in our driveway. Two Christian men loaded Mother's recliner and television into the back. Inside the house, I packed a suitcase with flannel nighties, two velour robes and slippers, some underwear and dresses, a pair of sturdy shoes. Deodorant, powder, hand lotion, and pill bottles fit into a corner.

"My pocketbook," Mother said urgently. "Be sure I have my pocketbook." I handed it to her. An old blue leather, her favorite, it was filled with white hairpins, loose pennies, and a hanky with lace edges, along with an old red wallet, bulging with snapshots, and containing a few dollars. She owned two new wallets, Christmas gifts from past years, but they always remained packaged and the familiar went with her. A giant print Bible, a calender of Florida scenes, and her glasses case also were packed.

The car door open, I waited, helping her settle into the front seat. Jim and Les had pulled away in the truck. I was glad. I didn't want to follow it on the expressway, our eyes fixed on those two pieces of furniture tied to the panels.

As I think back to that day, I am filled with wonder. In a matter of hours, I had talked with Mother, called our friends who had the truck, packed her belongings, and settled Mother in the room with Dad! With the decision made, all things fell into place as we made this drastic change in our lives.

That morning after breakfast I had helped Mother to her chair where she tried to read the paper, at least the headlines. I prayed as I approached her, knelt by her chair, and told her of my decision. "I just can't handle it any more, Mom," I said to her, my insides rubbery.

To my surprise, Mother looked straight at me. "You're tired," she nodded. "It's all right, Budsy" (a favorite nickname from childhood).

How God puts it all together for us when we truly seek His will and guidance. He knows the end from the beginning. That very day He knew that in a few brief months our daughter and her two small boys would be seeking shelter in our home.

Actually, some aspects of that day are not too clear in my memory. Mother's actual admittance, the unpacking and conferring with the staff, my encounter with an angry doctor I should have consulted first—all blend with the pleasant surprise on my father's face when he realized his wife of 52 years had come to share his space! "Now we can watch TV together in this motel!" he exclaimed. Dad's understanding of his accommodations ranged from being in a travelers' inn to a place where there were "inmates." His mind had begun to unravel, and during the next year I would be picking up the threads.

By now you may be asking, "How could you do that? I would feel so guilty! What did your husband say?"

At 5 o'clock I was back home preparing dinner when Bill walked in the door, threw his briefcase on the counter, and strode to the bedroom to change clothes. "Hi!" he hollered en route to his destination. Bill, six-foot-three, is not slow; every move is purposeful.

"Hi!" I called. In a few minutes Bill was back in the kitchen, a puzzled look on his face. "Where's Mother?"

"In the nursing home with Dad," I answered. Then I shared the events of the day. A man not easily rattled, Bill was flabbergasted. "You *what?*"

By the look on my husband's face I knew God's will had been accomplished. I may not recall all the details of the day, but I do remember the relief and surprise on his face, a relaxation of wrinkles, a clearness of eye that I had not seen for a long time.

To be honest and scriptural, I must admit I should have discussed this with my husband first, even though it was my mother and not his. But this was an unusual day. I know it was right because never once did I regret the decision I made the day I sat before God and put out a fleece.

Considering Priorities

Personally I feel that where a spouse is involved, we must prayerfully consider the situation of priority. Sometimes, of course, there is no other solution, particularly in a tight financial crunch; but those of us with spouses who suffer health problems must remember we could sacrifice their health, and even lives, under certain conditions.

This reminds me of Gladys, whom I met at a Christian Writers' conference. After the conference, she waited with me at the gate at O'Hare airport, since her plane did not leave for another hour. Her pale violet eyes and delicate skin were framed by softly curling white hair. Gladys' sweet spirit mixed with a gentle sadness had attracted me the first time we discussed our interests. Gladys wrote Sunday School leaflets for children. As a widow, she lived alone, surrounded by her daughter's family and dependent elderly relatives. "My mother lived with us from the time we were married," she offered softly. A little shocked to find out that her mother was only 54 at that time, I inquired about their relationship.

"Mother's hearing was extremely poor," she said. "And my husband said, 'Gladys, your mother will always have a home with us.' "

"You had a daughter. Did that cause any problems?"

"Not really. Of course, Mother was always there to do things around the house, so Susan didn't learn much about housekeeping."

"Did that bother you? I mean, did you feel your mother took over your place in the house?"

Gladys' voice was soft, slow. "Sometimes it did, but Mother was real good, easy to live with. And we had so many relatives living near us who needed help—my husband's and mine."

I moved closer to Gladys to avoid being jostled by travelers going everywhere and nowhere. Setting my briefcase on the floor and shading my eyes from a sudden burst of sunlight, I pressed on. "Did you and your husband ever feel a lack of privacy?"

It was harder now for Gladys to talk. She seemed to be listening to something. The noise of departing planes, the voices on the intercom, the crying of babies: none of these were sounds she heard. The sounds came from the past, perhaps. "At first it was all right," she said. "Mother was sensitive to our need to be alone, but as she grew older, she wouldn't leave us alone. I had to be very firm and insist, and then she would pout."

"That was hard for you, wasn't it?" Oh, there was something here I needed to know, and my plane was boarding!

"Yes, oh, yes. And now Mother's in a nursing home, and she was so glad I could come to this conference. But those other years. . . ." A rim of tears formed circles around the violet eyes. Then they splashed forth, finding little wrinkled crevices in which to lie.

"Those years," I said quickly. "What years?" I picked up my briefcase, boarding pass ready.

"My husband has been dead for five years now." The softness was still in her eyes as she said, "Oh, how I wish I had spent more time with him and less with Mother!"

I embraced Gladys one last time, sorry that I had uncovered her pain, but knowing it was therapeutic for her and helpful to me to share with others. Up the ramp I hurried, thinking I might never see this dear lady again.

Gladys told me her husband reminded her that anything they did for others was done for Jesus. "If you do it to the least of these my brethren, you do it unto Me" (Matt. 25:40, KJV). Doing the will of God in honoring our parents and caring for them requires a balance. There is also the injunction concerning marital status: to leave parents to be joined to a spouse (Eph. 5:31). And if single, a life of service to Him may not include care of a parent. It may be a matter of priorities.

Sorting True Guilt from False

If you are in a similar crisis, you may be confused, haunted, or disturbed by different factors. Perhaps you promised a parent that you would never put him or her in a nursing home. Phrased that way, it indicates abandonment—and abandonment of a parent *should* cause guilt. Effectively dealing with the trauma of care by entering a parent into the best facility you can locate should not cause guilt, provided you follow through with your responsibilities. Honoring a parent includes a willingness to love, share, listen to, and respect that person, no matter what his state of health or dependency. Honoring means praying for your parent. It does not mean being a doormat, dealing with the parent's demands to the exclusion of others' needs, or your own. If under duress you made such a promise, and you feel duty bound, I suggest you first pray alone, then counsel with your pastor or other mature Christian, preferably someone who has been in the same situation and reacted in a stable manner. Discuss it with your spouse.

Often married men, whose parents are living with them, leave most of the work and parent-relating to wives, and this can cause serious marital difficulty. A husband's mother is his responsibility and his wife will appreciate his interest and concern in the personal aspects, not just the financial and practical.

One great-grandmother of my acquaintance, who died at 102, defiantly dared her son to "put her away." For 10 years this strong-willed lady harassed her son in his own home, almost drove her daughter-in-law to a breakdown, and browbeat every aide they hired to help with her care. One evening we saw this woman and her son and daughter-in-law in a restaurant. This tiny lady of 90 pounds yanked her son away from us as he tried to converse. She behaved like a spoiled child of three, but the son allowed his mother to treat him this way. It was only after her 100th birthday, bedridden and mentally unstable, that she entered a nursing home.

Showing Compassion

In this era of child abuse, we also hear about physical abuse of parents. It is more common (even among Christians) to relate to a parent in a way that is emotionally abusive, perhaps without even knowing it. To replace that kind of abuse with compassion is vital.

> Compassion makes us see beauty in the midst of misery, hope in the center of pain. It makes us discover flowers between barbed wire and a soft spot in a frozen field. Compassion makes us notice the balding head and decaying teeth, feel the weakening handgrip and the wrinkling skin, and sense the fading memories and slipping thoughts, not as a proof of the absurdity of life, but as a gentle reminder that "a grain of wheat remains a solitary grain unless it falls into the ground and dies; but if it dies, it bears a rich harvest" (John 12:24, NEB) (Henri J. M. Nouwen and Walter Gaffney, *Aging,* Image Books, p. 113).

No one answer is right for everyone when parent care decisions are made. All the factors of life must be included: health of members of the family, stability of the marriage relationship, effects on children living at home, finances, God's will at the time. The latter can be assessed only through a relationship with God, a life yielded to Him. Whether a parent is kept in his own home, our home, or a nursing home, compassion and caring are factors under our control with the help of the Holy Spirit, for He provides strength when we believe our endurance has reached its end.

Now is the time, wherever we are in life, to affirm a right relationship with God—not when we are up against difficult decisions and strained endurance, or have reached old age. Praise is a vehicle we can use to affirm this now. Kathryn Parker Knudson, a grandmother, expressed it this way:

> I have awakened. It is early. No one is stirring. My whole soul turns to God in worship and adoration. My body, oh,

it is miserable, dull; it feels stupid; it says it wants more sleep. My heart and mind are heavy. Living death ever haunts one's way, springing out at every turn, and in every quiet hour. But from all of these I was delivered long ago, the night I crossed the Red Sea, and so my soul is free to worship the One I love.

Welcome, sunshine, rain, snow, or howling storm—it does not matter. It is God's day. Welcome, joy or sorrow; welcome, sickness or health, abundance or lack, friend or foe, companionship or solitude, strength or weakness— what does it matter? My Heavenly Father orders my days— what comes or goes, all has been committed to Him. I have just one care, and that is that I rest in Him. I want to live this day for His glory—and how can He be glorified in me if I fuss and complain and grumble and sigh and moan and lament?

I am Thine, O beloved Lord, and Thou mine, and unto Thee I give thanks for everything. Thou hast put a song in my heart, and that is what the world shall hear from me today.

When we know the Lord in this way, we shall be content, wherever we live.

5

She Has Done What
She Could

"She has done what she could: she has anointed My body before-hand for the burial." Mark 14:8

One of my favorite accounts in the Gospels is the one about Mary anointing Jesus with costly perfume. It was six days before the Passover, and the disciples had gathered in Bethany at the home of Simon the leper. Whether it was "an unnamed woman" or Mary, the sister of Martha and Lazarus, who did the anointing, the account is the same in Mark and Matthew, even to the kind of perfume. It was nard, a very expensive fragrance imported from India. How Mary obtained this, when it was worth as much as a day laborer earned in a year, we do not know.

Consider the scene. As was the custom, Jesus and the disciples were lounging at the table, which was most likely filled with fine figs and pomegranates. The smell of delicately prepared fish probably whet their appetites, yet it was a tense time. The chief priests and Pharisees had given orders that if anyone knew where Jesus was they should report it. As He rested at the table, Mary approached Him, her loosened hair falling over her shoulders. She took the beautiful flask from her robe, quickly broke the seal, and began to pour the liquid over Jesus' head. No doubt those who watched gasped, but by this time Mary had tearfully and passionately poured the last drops over His feet. Then she wiped His feet with her hair, while tears mingled with the perfume. So powerful was the sweet aroma, that the smell of food had lost its pungency. By then the disciples were aware of the fact that her act of devotion had cost 300 denarii. Judas was not the only indignant disciple. Would not most men have considered this a waste? Jesus had always emphasized caring for the poor. But Jesus announced that her deed would be remembered whenever the Good News is preached. Jesus declared "she did what she could."

This is a comforting, freeing, and satisfying statement when we apply it to the care of aged parents. Mary could have wrung her hands, followed Jesus everywhere, worried about His future, His every need. She could have brought Him a plate of fruit, a specially prepared cake, and that would have indicated her caring. Perhaps she could have offered to wash His robe in the river, or run errands for His disciples. In one loving, dramatic moment she said it all: "I love you, Lord. I know, as well as You, what is ahead. Let me anoint You, my King, with my most precious possession."

Certainly, had she sold the perfume, many widows and orphans would have had a feast; perhaps lepers would have worn new robes; poor women with no cooking utensils would have had some vessels for their meager meals. Jesus knew that, but He also knew Mary's heart. She had put her life on the altar; she did not care if she was reported to the Pharisees.

Sharing Christ's Love

I am not advocating that we carelessly throw away money or possessions when they should be given to the poor; or that we become irrational givers without proper thought to stewardship. Those of us inclined to fret, worry, and fuss over our parents, doing small things to assuage feelings of guilt, need to learn that nothing we do for our parents is as important as sharing the love of Christ—our most "precious possession"—with them. If our parents are the ones who taught us of Christ's love they need to see the fruit of their teaching in our lives as we minister to them; however, many Christians have parents who do not know the Lord as Saviour. The leading of the Spirit is important as we minister Jesus' love and the Good News. Indeed, these are the only realities we can give them as life drains away. Once we grasp the truth of doing what we can, ministering to our parents becomes less emotionally wearing. Some parents' demands are so excessive that children who frantically respond to them become ill physically, emotionally, or both. Then they are no help to the aged person who need *them* most. It sometimes hurts to say no to a parent, a friend, or a child, but often it provides balance and wholeness for both parties. On the other hand, some parents demand so little, protesting that they are burdens, that adult children aren't sure when they are properly helping their loved ones. Both situations cause tension that needs to be faced and understood.

Dealing with Emotions

Forgetfulness and confusion of parents can result in unhealthy responses. I routinely visited my mother three times a week, so I was totally unprepared for the storm one afternoon when I entered her room and approached the bed where she was resting. Angrily she attacked me. "Where have you been? You haven't been here for a week!" Since she had appeared cheer-fully responsive two days earlier, I was deeply hurt. My father, far more confused, would often say, "I haven't seen you for three months!" But I could always kid around with Dad and bring him back to reality. Mother's attack on this particular day (which occurred some time after my father's death) startled me into anger and tears. I ran out of the room, down two flights of stairs, and sat in the lobby. I felt so depressed, so unappreci-ated, so weary, that I almost left for home. What did it matter, I thought, since she didn't know how often I came, if I came at all? I shut my eyes and said *Jesus.* Calmness flowed through my body, removing anger and hurt. After several minutes of prayer, I returned to the room. I asked the aide to get Mother up in her chair. Neither of us discussed the incident, though I could see she remembered it. "I was here Tuesday," I defensively told her. But what did that matter? Tuesday, Thursday, Friday—they were all alike to her amid a tiresome routine. It's impor-tant to try to inject change into their days.

"Let's go outside," I suggested. "There's a lovely breeze."

There is no substitute for God's healing of emotions when such incidents occur. Forgiveness of one another is necessary, but it's sort of like bruising a knee: external ointment soothes; complete healing is slower and is accomplished only by the God-given healing properties of the body.

Whether it be guilt that comes from recognizing one's sin that needs to be healed by God, or only a neurotic response (that may require counseling), depression, physical ailments, and loss of energy often result. Not only do we feel the negative results in ourselves, but we show it in irritability and anger toward our families and even toward the staff at the medical facility where a parent is cared for.

Most staff persons at a good nursing home are trained to help the families of new patients as they seek to make this transition. Kay Newman, an R.N. whose love is geriatrics, was a charge nurse while my parents were patients. "It's very hard on families," she told me. "Some of them suffer guilt from the realization that they neglected their parents in earlier years, and are suddenly faced with a very helpless parent who needs nursing home care. It's not unusual for the person to indict staff members for problems that are not our fault. For instance, one lady felt we had abused her mother because she suffered bone fractures. The real cause was osteoporosis. We were really extremely careful when we moved or turned her."

Kay's love for old people was reflected in her advice and admonition toward the aides and orderlies. "I tell them to give the kind of care they would like for their own parent."

Misdirecting Our Emotions

We need to recognize that guilt can cause us to do too much or too little for a parent, or it can cause us to misdirect our emotions toward others. If we are suffering from guilt in our parental relationships, it is time to look at our priorities and other responsibilities, including our jobs, spouses, children, friends, and churches. When guilt becomes so excessive that it intrudes on other aspects of our lives, we must establish priorities. Some find it helpful to write down priority and time-management lists. Each of us is unique in areas of energy levels and our needs for rest. Our biological time clocks must be adjusted to the added responsibility of being caregivers to parents. If parents expect too much, we must say, "I cannot do that."

Urgent or Important?

In her book *How Do You Find the Time?* Pat King, mother of 10 writes: "Every time the urgent is put first, the important takes second place!" (Aglow Publications, p. 101) Many items on the agenda of an elderly person appear urgent. We need not take care of what appears urgent in order to feel we are performing properly. Instead, having established our own priorities, we do the important. Then the urgent falls into its proper place or often disappears.

During the eight years that my parents required help and supportive care, life did not stand still for Bill and me, and it will not for you. Our years spewed forth such traumas as my major surgery, Bill's many hospitalizations for heart and pulmonary problems, the death of our daughter Claire's first two babies, the birth of our daughter Lesley's premature baby who spent almost two years in a body cast, the birth of a baby girl to our son and his wife while they were both still in high school. A few years later, Claire and her two little boys came to live with us temporarily; her husband's drinking, gambling, and abuse eventually flung their marriage into divorce.

Friends and acquaintances dealt with such heartaches as children into drugs, in prison, or suicidal; others with crippling illnesses, widowhood, or loss of jobs while they coped with the life endings of parents who had once sustained them. God is indeed faithful. When we truly know Him, He gives us joy and turns our mourning into dancing! Nothing is too hard for God; His arm is not shortened! We need to establish communion with God through Jesus Christ His Son as early in life as we can.

During a sermon entitled "Our Comforting God," our pastor, Lowell B. Sykes, said:

> Life has a way of falling apart. We get one situation straightened out and something else comes up to plague us. Again, the aggravation is illustrated in the old cartoon of the Three Stooges in which they are trying and trying to get

the top drawer of a dresser closed. They struggle with it and finally it bangs shut. But as it does, the bottom drawer pops out and hits them in the shins! That's the way life is. Sometimes we can laugh at it, but many times we cannot and we sob with frustration, "Lord, how long can I stand this? One thing after another!"

Later in the same sermon, he said:

The things that perhaps you wish most had never been a part of your life—had never happened to you—as they are given to God, can be the very bridges over which you can bring compassion and comfort into another's life. If you had never known that failure, if you had never experienced that sin, if you had not been close to that particular death, if that depression had not settled on you like a black cloud, if you had not been through the anguish of that physical pain, you would never have any idea what a person is going through who had experienced those things.

We do what we can with what we have. When Jesus is first in our lives, we know we are forgiven and can forgive others. When we learn to cope with the many difficult situations in our lives, we can indeed affirm Paul's expression: "Blessed be the God and Father of our Lord Jesus Christ, the Father of mercies and God of all comfort, who comforts us in all our affliction so that we may be able to comfort those who are in any affliction with the comfort with which we ourselves are comforted by God" (2 Cor. 1:3).

6
Being Worthy

"He who loves father or mother more than Me is not worthy of Me; and he who loves son or daughter more than Me is not worthy of Me." Matthew 10:37

One of the most frequently asked questions by adult children concerning aging parents goes like this: "My 82-year-old mother's driving skills have deteriorated drastically and I'm worried that she may have an accident. When I hint that she should give up driving, she gets angry. What can I do?"

This question, and an answer, appeared in *Dynamic Years,* a magazine for working Americans in their middle years. "There is no particular age limit to tell an elderly person when to give up driving," says Al Lauersdorf, administrator of highway safety for the National Safety Council in Chicago. He continues:

> It's always a very touchy issue. Let your mother know she is endangering not only her safety, but the safety of

others. Sometimes a clergyman, physician, or trusted contemporary can do the job better than a son or daughter. If your mother insists on continuing to drive, advise her to stay off expressways where there is fast-moving traffic, and to drive only in daylight hours. Find out if there is public transportation near her home. Also, many communities have organizations that provide bus service. Let your mother know you will be available to drive her during a specified day and time each week ("Questions You've Asked," July-Aug. 1982).

Just as teenagers often drive too fast, elderly people frequently drive too slow. Both endanger other motorists and pedestrians. Owning and driving a car are the last activities elderly persons wish to relinquish, yet they react differently. Some assess their own situations and decide to drive only for short distances and not at night. Others are angry and defensive or give up in resentment and expect instant auto service from friends and relatives.

My father drove his Cadillac from New York to Virginia till he was in his late 80s. He was a good driver with excellent vision. During one trip, the car was hit broadside by a motorist who ran a stop sign. Mother and Dad managed to drive their damaged vehicle 90 miles back to Utica, buy a new one, turn around the next day, and continue their trip! Understandably, when they sold their home and moved to Virginia, Dad (at 90) was unwilling to sell his car and quit driving, but the shock of moving and his advanced age caused a rapid deterioration in his driving ability. When I suggested he make this change, Dad balked. Then one day during a routine medical checkup, I spoke privately to the doctor about my concern. In our case, the doctor proved to be the intermediary.

As we drove home, Dad remarked, "The doctor says my arm is too lame to continue driving. He called it *taxi driver's arm*. I told him I had driven trucks for years. I guess it's better if I give up driving."

Instead of telling Dad he was too old, slow, or inefficient, the doctor gave him an acceptable reason. Later, when Dad's arthritic arm hurt, he remembered that. "Good thing I stopped driving," he would say.

Financial Decisions

Other areas of concern to me were Dad's management of his finances and the possibility of his suddenly becoming incapacitated. Mother was not authorized to cosign checks or other documents. For years she had asked him to simplify his investments. Mother always did the bookkeeping for the business, but Dad alone managed the money and made all financial decisions. After talking to a lawyer, I asked my father if he would be willing to give me power of attorney, promising that I would not exercise it unless truly necessary. He had always trusted me, and in this case, having no brothers or sisters simplified matters; but Dad was adamant: the answer was *no*.

It is usually necessary for the one writing the checks, paying the bills, and sorting the insurance and Medicare claims to have power of attorney. In cases where there are many brothers and sisters, a meeting or telephone conference call may be needed— perhaps with an attorney present. When my father finally agreed (not happily) to give me this legal right, we signed the papers and I promptly put them away. One day they would be needed quickly. Till then, I allowed Dad to struggle along doing his own finances.

A cousin in her 60s discovered that her father, who lived alone and suffered from dementing illness, was stashing his

Social Security checks under the mattress and hiding hundreds of dollars in the kitchen cupboards and refrigerator. Finally, against his will, he was moved to a private home, whose caregivers understood him and provided him with a homelike atmosphere and good country cooking.

A friend told me that her father waited till all the family had left for work, then he fried cabbage (which he was not supposed to eat), leaving burned pans and smoke behind. He was scolded repeatedly, but continued to act defiantly and repeat his cooking till finally he was hospitalized for heart and kidney failure.

Role Reversal
Role reversal may be an overworked term, but how do we say it better? Once these fathers helped us with math, gave us allowances, and said no when we wanted to use the family car. Mothers made us brush our teeth and change our dirty clothes. Now *we*, their children, make these decisions for *them*.

Sometimes a parent makes the obvious solution difficult. In thinking through the problem, I realized that my love for them, my sense of duty, my desire to ease the responsibilities they had formerly borne, only served to cement them more firmly to the walls of their past. Their generation of Christians, so rooted in the law and ethics of the Old Testament, had struggled frugally, and faithfully executed duties foreign to many young people today. To have a daughter insist on change of any kind provoked them to anger, and even despair.

Fear of Disapproval
Mother's attachment to her family—even her ancestors—was so deeply rooted that she couldn't part with possessions that various family members had owned. Some articles were indeed valuable; others were plainly rubble. Even after moving twice,

our garage looked as though we were storing materials and furniture for an entire community. Bill and I decided to sell some of the furniture that remained, and add the income to the estate. My own reluctance to deal with such matters showed me I still suffered from fear of disapproval, a characteristic probably more common to only children.

As our parents age, and as we age, there needs to be a tension accommodation, a sincere effort to see the other person's position. Mother's life had really revolved around one area of the country, and a large family who had settled there. They visited and accumulated, married, buried, and depended on one another as members of a tight-knit community. Though she could not tell me what to do with these possessions, neither could she let go enough to approve of their disposal. It was seemingly an unsolvable matter.

In Psalm 39:6 we read, "Surely every man walks to and fro—like a shadow in a pantomime; surely for futility and emptiness they are in turmoil; each one heaps up riches, not knowing who will gather them" (AMP).

Not having our own houses in order presents others with the difficulty of disposal. There is indeed a balance needed here. We read in 1 Corinthians, "And those who deal with this world—overusing the enjoyments of this life—let them live as though they were not absorbed by it, and as if they had no dealings with it. For the outward form of this world—the present world order—is passing away" (7:31, AMP).

This last passage is more pertinent today, perhaps, than in any other period of history. World unrest, terrorism, hunger, toppling governments, and financial collapse everywhere we may look suggest to us that personal possessions be of low priority and that we obey our Lord's command to "occupy till I come" (Luke 19:13, KJV).

Seeking the Kingdom

Mother did not have her mind only on the treasures of earth, however. Some passages of Scripture were puzzling to her, and as she grew older, and closer to the Lord, she desired answers. One day we had a discussion about the Second Coming, and I read several passages of Scripture to her. She was most puzzled about Jesus' statement, "He who loves father or mother more than Me is not worthy of Me; and he who loves son or daughter more than Me is not worthy of Me." These words in Luke disturbed her even more: "If any one comes to Me and does not hate his [own] father, and mother [that is, in the sense of indifference to or relative disregard for them in comparison with his attitude toward God] and likewise his wife and children and brothers and sisters [yes] and even his own life also, he cannot be My disciple" (24:26, AMP).

From a commentary we also got this help: "The Gospel deepens human love, and often natural affection and loyalty to Jesus are compatible (Luke 18:20; Matt. 15:4-9), but when there is a conflict, the claims of Jesus come first. Jesus' followers, therefore, should not be moved by mere emotion or motivated by easy hopes" (Donald G. Miller, *The Layman's Bible Commentary, Luke,* Vol. 18, John Knox Press, pp. 118-119).

Where those emotions lead and how we view the *idols* of our lives is crucial to our own aging process and the *tension of accommodation* between us and our own children as we age. Jesus said to seek first His kingdom and His righteousness and all these things would be added (Matt. 6:33). I suspect He knew that when the hearts of His followers were first on the kingdom, "all those things" would be fewer and less important.

Life has a way of removing the worldly from us. Houses are torn down to make way for shopping malls, investments fail, possessions burn, are stolen, or delegated to someone else, but

Jesus Christ is the same yesterday, today, and forever! (Heb. 13:8)

Being Worthy Now

Our renewal in the Spirit promises power and victory, not only when we eventually join the circle around the throne, but in the here and now. Singing to the Lord and praising Him with prayer and Scripture feeds our spirits as we seek to be worthy of our calling as disciples.

How can we live as though this life will never end—accumulating, idolizing, closing our ears to the call of the Spirit? We do it, impatient, fractious, possessive people that we are, no different from the Israelites throughout biblical history.

If and when we hear God's call and understand His leading, how do we put it first, our love for parent and child? Wisdom and balance are required as we seek to be worthy of Jesus.

When Jesus told the man to follow Him and not take the time to go back and bury his father, I hear Him saying: "If you wait till all your earthly duties are discharged to come and follow Me, the time may not come for you. You'll miss the kingdom. Put Me first, ahead of the demands of parent and child."

We all have places in the body of Christ, exercising our gifts and following our callings. God does not expect us to abandon these callings, though He may change our directions. That is why studying and listening are such vital parts of our faith.

Meeting Parents' Changing Needs

Some aged parents expect Christian children to abandon callings or lifestyles in order to accommodate the parents' changing needs. A parent may want to keep a home, to hold on to his holdings and independence, and cannot always see the disruption he causes in his children's lives (including fighting among siblings). We, as these children, need the balance of honoring parents without dropping our own lives, which have been ordered by God, in order to pick up theirs.

To be effective servants in role reversal, calls for willingness to:

• *Accept what has happened.* Wishing will not push back time. Wasting energy on regret over past decisions, poor choices, or failures is futile. Affirm the time. It is today. Go on from here.

• *Accept our personhood.* We are precious to God. He understands the responsibilities in our lives—our marital status, our jobs, our financial and health requirements. We *do* need rest and change; our parents are not our only responsibility. All that appears urgent is not necessarily important. Time for renewal and rest are vital to being effective servants in the kingdom.

• *Accept our parents' personhood.* Whatever illness of mind or body a parent has suffered, he or she is precious to God. That he can no longer function independently or as well as he did in his earlier years, does not make him any less valuable to God. Praise is as important to growth in old age as it is for children. Small improvements and achieved goals encourage the old as well as the young. Contrary to statistics, some old people are able to learn new skills, revive old interests, and more importantly, accept the Lord Jesus as personal Saviour.

• *Accept counseling.* Some of us think because we are Christ's disciples, we don't need help. Our emotions, misunderstandings, and deep-seated hurts sometimes combine to make it difficult or impossible to function properly as caregivers to parents. If this happens, feel free to acknowledge it and seek counsel from a pastor, a trusted friend, or even an adult child. Expressing pain or getting another's perspective can break the stalemate and move us forward.

The Lord Himself is my inheritance, my prize. He is my food and drink, my highest joy! He guards all that is mine. He sees that I am given pleasant brooks and meadows as my share! What a wonderful inheritance! I will bless the Lord who counsels me; He gives me wisdom in the night. He tells me what to do. I am always thinking of the Lord; and because He is so near, I never need to stumble or to fall. Heart, body, and soul are filled with joy. For You will not leave me among the dead; You will not allow Your beloved one to rot in the grave. You have let me experience the joys of life and the exquisite pleasures of Your own eternal presence" (Ps. 16:5-11, TLB).

7
My Complaint Is Rebellion

"Then Job replied, 'Even today my complaint is rebellion; His hand is heavy despite my groaning. Oh, that I knew where I might find Him, that I might come to His seat!'" Job 23:1-3

"And the people spoke against God and Moses, 'Why have you brought us up out of Egypt to die in this wilderness? For there is no food and no water, and we loathe this miserable food.'" Numbers 21:5

I heard quiet laughter coming from my parents' room at the nursing home. Then my son's cheery voice. "It was such fun, Grandma. Baskets and baskets of 'em. Of course I ate more than I brought to the house!"

Grandma leaned closer to hear him better. "You helped me stir the jam, remember?" she asked.

Grandpa's head lifted. "I'd like some of that jam now, Mother," he said.

"Wish I could do it. I'm no good for anything anymore."
Wayne, her grandson, reached for her hand. "Oh, now, Grandma,
don't say that. We love you. Just remember I haven't forgotten
those good times I had at your house!"

Strawberries, of course. That was the topic. Adult grandchildren have a way of lifting spirits through reminiscing that we,
as the children, do not. As soon as Mother saw me, she squinted,
lowered her chin and grouched about her dinner. "Look! Who
could eat *that?*"

I looked at the plate on her tray, its untouched Swiss steak
cut into small pieces. I took a bite.

"It's tough!" Mother said. "Tough!"

I didn't think so, but I had all my own teeth. I turned to my
son. "Sounds like you and Grandma were having a good time."
Wayne gave his grandmother a kiss and announced he was off
to work.

One of our daughters lived in the same city and visited too.
She and my mother always had a special relationship; some sort
of generational chemistry existed between them. "She was a
special grandma," Claire told me. Even in her 70s my mother
picked berries with the children, made play spaces for them in
the garage, and allowed them to help with cookies. Now it was
hard for the grandchildren to watch her feeble attempts at
walking, those painfully swollen legs clumping along like inani-
mate pillars.

Often we hear that grandparents get all the fun with the
children and the parents get the work. When we assist an aged
parent, we get the work, and the grandchildren get the fun.
They visit, listen to stories with relish, bring a gift, and then
with a smile dash away until the next time. Complaints are
reserved for the adult child.

Dealing with Complaints

Nursing parents at home or visiting them regularly, hearing their complaints about care, meals, inability to function as they used to: all this accentuates recognition of our own aging. Erma Bombeck wrote about looking down at her hands and seeing that they were her mother's. Right at the time when parents need our help the most, we are experiencing change ourselves—physical problems (often the beginning of the same ones we see in our parents), career or retirement transitions, widowhood, reduced income, pressure from children needing financial help or who have returned to the nest, and even caring for grandchildren. Because the physical and emotional strain at this time underscores our own aging, we often feel rebellious. Resentment may build toward a parent whom we perceive to be the cause of our present condition. Dr. Archibald D. Hart says, "When unresolved anger is experienced over a period of time, it creates in us a feeling of displeasure and indignation which is called resentment" (*Feeling Free*, Fleming H. Revell, p. 89).

To resolve these feelings we must first acknowledge them. If we don't, the anger and resentment increase and cause constant friction in the relationship with a parent.

We must recognize that a parent may have no other outlet for his or her frustration. Though we may be able to share our feelings with a spouse or a friend, most parents put up a good front to visitors, whether they are friends, pastor, or relatives from other areas who visit briefly. They save their discouragement, complaints, and hostility for their children.

We need to forgive our parents. Forgiveness is not necessarily for some recent incident. We may need to forgive another for an action causing longstanding resentment in us. Because I had so much responsibility for both parents, I recognized that I needed to forgive my mother for having an only child. Many years before, Mother told me she had decided not to have more children. As a little girl, I used to pretend I had an older brother who was away at school; sometimes I "talked" to a pretend sister. Though I always felt loved and wanted, I longed for siblings. This is an interesting thought today when many couples are putting off raising families or planning to have only one child. According to statistics, only children are generally more intelligent, healthier, and have more opportunities for education and development than those from large families. This may be true, but I believe that growing up with brothers or sisters has advantages.

On days when I felt particularly weary, I dwelt on the fact that I had no brother or sister with whom to share concerns. One day, while meditating, the Lord showed me my need to forgive my mother. I wrote the date in my journal. Then, whenever Satan reminded me of my resentment, I stood my ground. "On this particular date," I would say, "I forgave Mother for making me an only child." In time, the resentment left and a deeper love for my mother was a reward for that time of forgiveness.

You may say, "That was a simple thing to forgive, but I had a father who beat me whenever he came home drunk." Or, "I had a mother who disappeared for days at a time." It is true some parents have hurt us physically or emotionally in terrible ways, yet it is not the degree of hurt that we measure when we forgive a parent. God used no such yardstick when He sent His only Son to die for us. Willingness to forgive a parent, and consistently affirming the decision, eventually results in truly being able to love that father or mother, in feeling more relaxed, more energetic, and better able to carry out duties, to sleep better, and have fewer physical ailments. Forgiveness is purifying, and eliminates the regret that accompanies a lack of forgiveness when it is too late.

Dealing with Demands

Mother's demands on my time, especially while she was living with us, were often picayune and excessive. She might call me from one end of the house in the midst of a difficult chore just to have me see a particular person in a soap opera. Or she might keep changing her mind about what she wanted for lunch even though I had it prepared. She would call me to cover her legs with her afghan, a task she was capable of doing for herself. No wonder I felt resentful and weary! But whose fault was that? Not Mother's. That was my problem, and I did not take a stand.

One night I had a dream that expressed this problem. It is well to record a dream immediately before you forget it. Through it you may learn truths about yourself and your relationships, answers to problems, and perhaps hear from God in a creative way. In this particular dream, Mother and I had gone to a Christian Women's Club luncheon (which we often did while she was still able to go out) and had left the table to go to a rest room. I was guiding Mother, holding her arm just as I always did. The rest room, located on an upper floor, looked out over a large parking lot, and I could see my car parked at the farthest corner of the lot. Mother pointed out the window and said in a gentle voice, "Would you go out to the car and get me a little glass of goat's milk?"

Even in the dream, I felt resentment rising. Here I had taken her to a nice luncheon but she was not satisfied! She wanted me to walk all the way out to the car for a glass of goat's milk! To get goat's milk symbolized her preposterous requests. Just as I was about to "let her have it," a woman smilingly said to me, "The word for today is *kindness!*"

When I awakened, I could still hear her bell-like voice. *Kindness!* "But when the Holy Spirit controls our lives He will produce this kind of fruit in us: love, joy, peace, patience, kindness, goodness, faithfulness" (Gal. 5:22, TLB).

Learning the Firm *No*

As I meditated on this dream, I could see that my response to preposterous demands need not be anger or rebellion. If the Holy Spirit was in control of my life, the response could be patient and kind; it could also be a firm *no*.

"No, I am busy now. You may come get yourself a glass of milk if you wish."

"I cannot write that letter today. I'll do it for you tomorrow."

"Is there anything you need now? I shall be busy for the next couple of hours and can't be disturbed."

Why was it hard for me to assert myself, to be firm, to say no? I believe because Mother never let me forget she was giving up so much to move, I tried to replace all those things—friends and family, church, home, furniture—by responding to her unreasonable and frequent demands. I am sure Mother herself was unaware of her anger at no longer being in control of her life. Unfortunately, both of us lost our natural zest for living during this trying time.

Maturity coupled with kindness effected a dramatic change in the 93-year-old mother of a friend. This aged mother, who had been living in another state with her daughter, came to spend some time with her son Dick, who is 70, and her daughter-in-law, Jean, age 65. Evidently the daughter harbored bitterness and rebellion in her heart, as she had yelled at her mother constantly, told her off and, in general, behaved rudely toward her. This elderly lady was able to walk, perform simple tasks, and converse rationally; but she was weak, undernourished, and depressed when she arrived.

She was given nutritious meals and a sensible routine. Her person was respected by these two elderly people who were caring for her and within a few weeks a noticeable change in her had occurred.

As I turned to leave their home one day, Jean told me, "She wants to stay." Of course. Aged people respond to the same sort of care that young children do—love, good food, routine, and discipline.

If a parent comes to live in your home, *begin right* and you will have less cause for guilt, rebellion, and resentment on both sides.

• *We cannot replace the husband or wife of a parent.* A recently widowed parent will be lonely, but we cannot help that loneliness by attempting to replace the one who has died. The desires and interests of our own spouses come first, regardless of the parent's loss. We must be firm about needing privacy. Speaking the truth in love may not be well-received, but that is the parent's problem, not ours.

• *Be a helper, not a slave.* A medical examination of a parent will help to assess real needs. We have not been hired as nurse-companions. We are daughters or sons or in-laws who are willing to help when necessary, to encourage independence when possible. Some parents, however, refuse to be helped at all, and therefore do not bathe or dress properly. Firmness is needed, as well as reminders. Give encouragement and praise for the things they do well.

• *Prepare the parent's room in a practical way.* Using some of a parent's own furniture enhances feelings of security. Arrange lighting to best advantage and install a night-light. Hang a bulletin board for pictures and reminders. Throw rugs are dangerous. Since many old people fall out of bed, a bed rail is often a help. Remove a lock that is installed on the inside of the door to prevent the aged parent from locking you out when you might be needed in an emergency.

• *Have rules.* Even if this is painful, rules are as necessary in these circumstances as they are for the benefit of children. In our homes, parents must follow family routines, not expecting help at inconvenient times unless it is unavoidable. Be clear in explaining mealtimes, entertaining, and the rights of children who may be living at home. If the parent's health permits, encourage sewing, reading, doing crafts, dusting the room, and looking at some TV. Place a comfortable chair outside during pleasant weather, and invite an older friend occasionally to visit alone with a parent.

• *Decisions: Most are ours.* If a parent is ailing enough to need our help at home, he probably needs us to make decisions concerning finances, doctor appointments, and daily routines. Allow a parent to make small decisions, such as choice of subscriptions to magazines, clothing purchases, and snack choices. If parent care becomes too stressful, consider the options: a nursing home, having the parent visit another relative for a break, or hiring part-time help. Another alternative is to work outside the home and hire full-time help.

Life together in those last years need not be one of frequent conflict. Times of pleasure and joy often break forth spontaneously; other times they need to be planned. It is healthy and fulfilling to find common ground that fosters harmony in the family group.

Before my parents were in those last stages of life, they enjoyed family gatherings, watching great-grandchildren fly kites, eating ice cream on the patio, patting the family pets, singing hymns and Gospel songs as Bill played his autoharp. Reading psalms of praise erased fretfulness and sadness. Having friends in for tea or a snack provided outside stimulation. Giving parents a chore to do—such as preparing vegetables or cracking nuts—provides help and a sense of usefulness for them.

Asking parents to forgive when we have been irritable and short-tempered smooths the day. Be real. Let go of the past. To give the present and the future to the Lord sounds simplistic, but we can actively will to help ourselves and our parents. "And above all these (put on) love and enfold yourselves with the bond of perfectness—which binds everything together completely in ideal harmony" (Col. 3:14, AMP).

8
Light My Candle

"For Thou wilt light my candle; the Lord my God will enlighten my darkness." Psalm 18:28, KJV

"He who has the Son has life: He who does not have the Son of God does not have life." 1 John 5:12

Florence Snethen, a resident of a nursing home in Eau Claire, Wisconsin, is 93 years old and writes poetry. The Lord has been her light for many years. Though her mother died when she was 7 and she lived in an orphanage or with relatives, her poetry reflects compassion, humor, and acceptance.

Florence's insight into life's vicissitudes is expressed in *Finished Product.*

> Moving down an assembly line
> A beautiful car came through
> Many workmen were involved;

They knew just what to do—
So it is with a human life;
    Many people have a part
Parents, preachers, friends, and teachers
    To give one the fresh start.
As with a car, a well-built life
    Through the fault of some careless one
Though it had careful workmanship
    It may quickly be undone
'Tis far better to avoid a wreck
    No matter who's to blame—
Although man and car may be repaired
    They are never quite the same.

While science and medicine work laboriously to lengthen the human life span and to solve the mysteries of such diseases as cancer and Alzheimer's, many churches are behind in ministering to their elderly. Though churches have Golden Oldie clubs, Keenagers, and Ageless Wonders, a satisfying program of worship and study is not always given priority over bus trips, crafts, and speakers. All these should be provided, but the depth of need in the lives of people like Florence Snethen is seldom met.

People over 90 are no longer a rarity. In fact, statistically, those who survive their 50s and 60s are much more likely to live beyond 85 than the population as a whole.

Two of my father's cousins, now in their 90s, still write to me. One finished her last letter with this quip: "I was 91 in April and felt fine until I had the fall, but I am working for a comeback. Listen, Dearie, I still have all my teeth. How's that?" This plucky oldster lives alone in her own home. Irene, another cousin, a former schoolteacher and now a nursing home resident, has outlived four pacemakers and writes: "You don't know how terrible it is to grow old and be good for nothing. I can't see why the Lord doesn't take me as long as my heart is so bad. I hope you can read this terrible writing. At 94 it is a wonder I can write at all."

Sharing the Gospel

Actually, Irene's writing is more legible than mine, and her mind keen. Though she suffers from painful arthritis, she can still read and has asked me theological questions that no one has discussed with her. If science is going to provide the Irenes of our world with pacemakers and pills, then we, the church, should be far more active in sharing with them the Gospel of Christ and how He meets us where we are.

Those who say, "I have a private faith" or, "I don't talk about my religion," certainly have no biblical basis for such an attitude. It's not the way to turn the world upside down as the early Christians did (Acts 17:6).

Ruth, a tiny lady of 84 years, was a patient at the same nursing home as my parents. She had lived most of her life in New York State, but her later years were spent in Florida with her retired doctor husband. A widow, Ruth was frail and barely able to walk, even with help. The first time I saw her, she was reading a paperback from the accumulation of novels neatly stacked beside two pink flowering plants on her windowsill. Ruth had soft white skin over small bones, and wore a ruffled, lace-trimmed pink gown. Her lap robe was white sprinkled with pink roses.

During my frequent visits to Mother and Dad, Ruth and I exchanged polite conversation. Though her mind was alert, there was an aloofness or detachment—perhaps even depression. I continued to visit Ruth occasionally. I noticed a gradual change, a gentle fading. She was served a protein drink, as she often refused to eat.

One day while I was praying at home, the Lord seemed to ask a question: Have you told Ruth about Me? A little startled, I realized I had never shared my faith or prayed with this elderly lady. In spite of all the paperbacks around her bed, I never saw a Bible.

When I visited the following day, Ruth sat in her usual chair, a closed paperback in her lap. Pale blue eyes watched me as I moved close and sat on her bed. After the general questions had been asked, I took her hand. "Ruth, have you ever accepted Jesus Christ as your Lord and Saviour?"

There was a short silence, followed by her soft answer. "No, I don't think I ever have."

"Would you like to?"

Her voice was low, steady, and even a little eager as she replied, "I would. Yes, I believe I would."

"No one can do it for you, Ruth. He is waiting, but you must yield your heart."

"No, no one can do it for you," Ruth repeated. Then, her eyes closed, one tear slowly running down her cheek, she prayed aloud, telling the Lord what He had been waiting to hear. During the following two weeks we spent time in prayer together.

Three weeks later Ruth slipped into a coma. I knelt beside her bed and told her how much she meant to me. I read her the encouraging words of David, the promises of Jesus. There was no response, but I felt she heard.

Never Too Late

One day I stopped in and the bed was empty. There were no books or flowers on the windowsill. The pink gowns had disappeared from the closet. I had learned a lesson. It may be too late to learn to ride a bicycle or play tennis; too late to learn to drive, to garden, or to swim; but while we still have the gift of life, it is never too late to give ourselves to the Lord. I believe God had waited for Ruth's answer to Him, and then He graciously took her home.

If you are open and compassionate it will be difficult to restrain your witness to patients in a medical facility. I do not mean to suggest that you wave your Bible and whirl them around in their wheelchairs! As you visit, you will become sensitive to particular people, and the Spirit will show you individual needs.

I met Doris, a prayer warrior, at an intercessors' conference. She told me how she had become a catalyst between her friend Laura and Laura's mother, a nursing home patient with a broken hip. Laura had spent 10 years in a mental institution. She had been released, but her complete recovery was blocked by her mother complaining and accusing her. The mother said to her daughter, "People say I don't look like I belong here!" to which Laura replied, "People said that of me when I was in the mental institution, Mother."

The Lord gave Doris His wisdom as she visited this mother, showing her that the resentment over her confinement was harming her daughter who was the only member of the family able to visit her.

I believe this illustrates a point for those of us who make occasional visits to patients in medical facilities. Our brief exchanges do not provide us with knowledge of the entire situation or "both sides of the story." A careless statement may undermine a family relationship that is hanging by a thread. We may agitate the patient or his family; we may promise hope that we are powerless to deliver.

One handsome elderly man, wearing a pinstriped shirt and a tie, usually sat in his wheelchair near the entrance of my parents' room. He seemed so accomplished, telling me extravagant stories of his past and present. I listened, assuming that he was wheelchair-bound due to a heart condition. How surprised I was to find one day that he had accosted a nurse with a knife and had escaped from the home! (They found him in a few minutes.)

Unless you have been involved for some time with geriatric patients, you may be surprised to find that a person who had responded to you and enjoyed your companionship suddenly refuses to see you or does not know you. In cases like this, tell the staff about the change in this person: it may be symptomatic of a new illness or organic brain disease.

Visiting Other Patients

Not all patients in a nursing home are over 65. Accidents, muscle and nerve diseases, even strokes, render young people incapable of living independent lives. While my parents were hospitalized, Mike, a 22-year-old construction worker, struggled with therapy, finally leaving for a rehabilitation center to learn a new type of skill that would enable him to be gainfully employed.

The unmistakable odor of roses greeted me one afternoon as I stepped out of the elevator at Medical Care Center. "Roses!" I blurted out, looking for the usual basket sent to the home by the family of a deceased patient.

"Right!" responded a nurse carrying a tray of medications. "Reba's husband sent them to every patient!"

Sure enough, every room was bursting with red blooms. Reba's husband, a florist, showed his caring in the only way he could. His infrequent visits to his wife, a woman about 50 with multiple sclerosis, left her exhausted and frustrated. Usually very quiet, one day she angrily shared with me her resentment toward her husband, tensing her fists and turning her head fretfully on the pillow. All I could do was hold her hand and listen. Reba died after three years in the medical center.

Sam, my father's first roommate, was 58 when brain damage occurred following heart surgery. He was attached to tubes and machines when I met him. Several of us prayed faithfully and praised the Lord as he gradually became independent of the technology that had sustained him. He began to eat, adding flesh to Ichabod-like bones. By the time both my parents had died, Sam was able to converse (though in limited ways), walk awkwardly, and spend a few holidays at home. Sometimes I wonder if we stopped praying too soon. Perhaps full recovery was in order. Thoughts such as these can complicate our own emotions and relationships. I decided I could not carry guilt over Sam.

One of the most difficult aspects of visiting a family member in a nursing home is that of visiting others too. I reached a place, for a time, when I could not do so: my own weariness rendered me incapable of coherent exchange with other patients. Some families never visited other patients even though I knew them to be caring people. Perhaps their loved ones desired every bit of them, every moment they could spare. My mother seemed to feel this way, and I solved it by wheeling her chair into rooms where we would meet both patients and visitors, enhancing interpersonal communion for all of us.

Help in the Dying Process

I met Bertha McCray while she was a private duty nursing assistant for the patient in the room next to my parents. Eventually she would be the one who would nurse my mother through the dying process. I feel certain the Lord put her in my path early so that we could become acquainted.

Doctors trusted Bertha. Her intelligence, expertise, Christian love, and sense of purpose for her own life were evident as she nursed her patients—usually the terminally ill and very elderly. She herself was elderly—a mother and grandmother of many, rightly proud of the accomplishments of her grown children. Soft-spoken and warm, yet efficient, Bertha's long experience with the dying gave her a wisdom and balance for dealing with the families of her patients. Jesus was truly her light: He lightened the darkness of death for many of her patients; and He lightened the grief of loved ones through her ministry.

Throughout her life Bertha had learned instinctively what is now taught: to recognize the various stages of death (denial, anger, bargaining, depression, acceptance); how to care for terminal patients who need the companionship of others during the dying process; how to watch for significant signs (which are not always noted by purely clinical observers).

Mother and Dad liked Bertha. She visited with us sometimes when her patient was sleeping, and often helped aides with Dad when he became obstreperous and unyielding. From this wise woman I learned much about love, patience, truth, and compassion.

Her commanding presence seemed to quiet unruly patients. They recognized her as an authority figure as well as a nurse. Bertha's Christian witness to others was the life she led and a tenderness that came from regular study of the Word.

"Am I on my last legs?" This was a question my mother asked half seriously, half in jest, each time she had a setback during her last two years of life.

"No, not yet!" I would reply, really not knowing when she would lie dying, voiceless, quiet.

After one hospitalization, when a cataract was removed from

her eye, Mother suffered a mild stroke, preventing completion of the surgery. But the doctor had removed the worst one first, so she did have partial eyesight after that.

"Am I on my last legs?" came that faint voice, after a fall that cracked her pelvis. Not waiting for an aide to help her to the bathroom, she had tried to go it alone, and failed.

"Just a couple of weeks flat on your back and then you'll be better—unless you try to walk alone again!" I smiled as I said it.

Dad's attitude during his last two years of life was a practical and thankful one. "I've lived a long time, and hardly ever been sick," he reasoned. Then with a sly glance he would direct his words to Mother. "I didn't drink, smoke, or run around with other women."

Mother answered dryly, "Well, I knew the first two. I'm certainly glad to hear the last one."

My father seemed to have no regrets, none that he talked about. Though his lifelong occupation was not the one of his choosing, he blamed no one and accepted the way his family had shaped his future. He married my mother, knowing he was her second choice. Her first fiancé, whose ring she wore throughout her marriage, was killed shortly before their wedding. Dad loved Mother very much, but his temper and demanding disposition clouded this love and produced havoc throughout a frequently stormy relationship. Yet they valued each other in a special way, traveling together, sharing some of the same interests.

Visits of Pastors

Dad seemed to be prepared for death, sure of his eternal future, needing only my frequent companionship and assurance. Both parents welcomed the visits of various pastors who came to share with patients from the Bible, and to pray with them. So pleasing was that to them that I encourage pastors who have the time (or make the time) to visit nursing homes. To that aged generation, often displaced from their home churches, visits by pastors are special.

As we are sensitive to the needs of dying parents or friends, we hear their faint cries for light. Sometimes it comes through physical pain or mental anguish; sometimes it is seen in faded eyes, or felt in a tired handclasp. Sometimes it is buried under superficial pastimes or reticence, as it was with Ruth. It is in most of us, if we are aware enough to know the time has come to move from our earth space to another place prepared for us. When we do not have the words ourselves, the Bible does. Comfort, truth, and assurance may be read to those whose candle is dimming.

"I am the Light of the world," said Jesus. And then He told us not to hide our light under a bushel. Our instructions are clear. The Holy Spirit gives us the wisdom to show that light. All we need to do is ask.

9
Forsake Me Not

"In You, O Lord, do I put my trust and confidently take refuge; let me never be put to shame or confusion! Cast me not off in the time of old age; forsake me not when my strength is spent and my powers fail." Psalm 71:1, 9, AMP

What pictures come to mind when you read the words "take refuge"? Do you think of a cave, a bomb shelter, a redwood tree, or the comforting wings of a mother hen? In meditating on this verse I see an open meadow, grass bending in the wind, sun beating down on a treeless plain. When we are helpless and unshielded, God can be our only protection. He is there when we are the targets of anger or criticism. We can have confidence in Him.

When we put our trust in God at an early age we build a foundation for knowing that in our late years, when our strength is spent and our powers fail, He will not fail us. The psalmist does not say that *our* strength will always be sufficient, or that *our* powers, physical or mental, will not fail; but that we may put our trust confidently in the Lord—and that means in old age too.

Dr. Laurence Crapo and Dr. Donald Fries, Stanford University medical professors, predict a longer life span for Americans. They forecast that medical science is on the verge of extending the span to 85, which is considerably beyond the current average of under 70 for men and 77 for women. Their study examines aging and how it is being drastically affected by medicine and techniques (*AARP Bulletin,* April 1982).

Unless these longer lives are sustained by trust in God, will there be satisfying improvement?

Learning about a Refuge

Entering the lobby of the nursing home one Thursday morning I heard voices repeating a poem in unison:

> Faith came singing into the room,
> And other guests took flight:
> Fear, anxiety, grief, and gloom
> Vanished into the night.
>
> I wondered how such peace could be,
> But faith said gently, "Don't you see
> They really cannot live with me."

I walked to the all-purpose room where the weekly Bible study was conducted by Rebecca Riviere, a lovely gifted Christian who had been a professional singer. Each week, after the group repeated their poem, Rebecca sang before opening the Word of God in an insightful way. A few, my mother included, could not grasp the teaching; but they soaked up the Word. The healing properties of Scripture quieted them and underscored their refuge in the Lord.

Quietly I left, thinking of the words of the poem.

Taking the elevator, I rode with a plump rosy-cheeked aide who was manipulating a wheelchair supporting an elderly lady. Vacant eyes looked up at me, wisps of gray hair fell over sunken cheeks. Clutched in her arms lay a baby doll, neatly gowned in embroidered lace and wrapped in a pink flannel blanket. I reached out and touched the doll. "How's your baby today?" I asked. I felt a catch in my throat as I remembered the time I had brought one of my grandchildren, a loving little boy, who climbed into Mrs. Nichol's lap.

"This is *my* baby," I had told her.

She touched Christopher's bare brown leg. "Oh, *your* baby is warm," she observed.

Soon after Mrs. Nichol received her "baby" several other dolls appeared on ladies' laps. As some of the women patients regressed in thought and speech, the dolls seemed to satisfy a yearning.

When Families and Faculties Fail

Never, during the years my parents were residents at the home, did I see a member of Mrs. Nichol's family. Perhaps they came. One Christmas, though, gift-wrapped boxes lay on her bedside chair, unopened. Late in the day, when Bill and I were returning Mother and Dad to the home after the holiday with us, I heard a nurse say, "Oh, Mrs. Nichol, your presents aren't opened. Come, I'll help you. Here, you pull the ribbon."

One day I arrived to visit Dad at lunchtime. He was concentrating on his tray, sprinkling two packets of powdered saccharin over his broiled chicken, baked potato, and green beans. He opened another packet, and covered his buttered bread and dish of dietetic peaches.

"Dad! You're putting sugar on your food!"

"Yep. Tastes better that way."

Mother was stirring her tea. "He always does that," she told me. "I think it's terrible. He's crazy."

He did indeed do it every day, since he did not use the sweetener in his coffee. Perhaps, as a diabetic, he craved sugar.

Once again, I thought about that poem Dad had composed almost 50 years earlier. This same man (who was now mixing his peaches with his beans) had once written:

> The inviting green cucumber
> Gets most everybody's number
> While the green corn has a system all its own;
> Though a radish seems nutritious
> Its behavior is quite vicious
> And a doctor will be coming to your home.

I sank wearily into the plastic chair near Dad's wheelchair. I noticed that the plants on his windowsill had died. I had tried to keep this retired florist supplied with plants, but I stopped when I discovered that the reason for their death was the nutrients they were receiving. Dad was watering them with the contents of his urinal.

It was a time when Holy Communion was celebrated in the dayroom, though, that showed me the extent of his mental deterioration. That day, as the wafer was being passed to a circle of patients, my father's face became strangely dark and melancholy. I knelt before him, offering the wafer. He pushed it away. I tried to place it in his mouth. He spit it out. Finally, when I put it in his hand, he tucked it in the pocket of his sweater, which he always wore over his pajamas. "Dad," I whispered, using words I thought he would recognize from his

Lutheran prayer book, "Bread of heaven, on Thee we feed, For Thy flesh is meat indeed: Ever may our souls be fed with this true and living bread." He became so agitated that I had to take him back to his room.

I do not pretend to understand his anger and rebellion. Alone in the rest room I wept tears of hurt and frustration. Had I hoped that participating in communion, so often a part of his past, would heal Dad's mind? Had I simply wanted to share in this communion with my aged father? Was it the shock of knowing that he was, in a sense, dead?

Is Your Father Dead?

The thought that a senile parent is *dead* is not the same as describing someone as a *vegetable* (a term I find distasteful and inappropriate). It was a totally new thought to me until a friend said one day in her frank way, "Is your father dead for you?"

Shocked, I heard myself answer, "Yes."

The first stage of death begins quietly and is graphically described by Paul Tournier in his book *Learn to Grow Old!*

> It is no easy matter to accept that one is growing old, and no one succeeds in doing it without first overcoming his spontaneous refusal. It is difficult, too, to accept the growing old of someone else, of one's nearest and dearest. That of a mother whose kindness, welcome, and understanding used to seem inexhaustible, and with whom one begins to hesitate to share one's intimate confidences, because they no longer arouse in her the warm, lively echo they used to. The aging of a father whose judgment and advice always used to seem so sound, but whom one can no longer consult because he must not be worried, or because his faculties are failing. The aging of a friend to whom one no longer talks as one used to, because it would

be necessary to shout loud things that used to be said quietly. It is hard to accept the decay of conversation into banality, empty optimism, and insignificance (Harper and Row, p. 165).

Senile dementia—that's how the doctor described my father's irrational and sometimes inexplicable behavior. The meaning of the words is obvious, but there are many specific types such as Alzheimer's disease, which must be professionally diagnosed. Named for a German neurologist who first described it in 1906, Alzheimer's is an irreversible brain disorder and the fourth leading cause of death among adults. It brings gradual deterioration of memory and intellectual abilities, eventually requiring full-time nursing care. Scans and X rays of the brain are essential to differentiate this form of *senile dementia* from depression, anxiety, delusion, cardiovascular problems, or the effects of malnutrition or medication.

Dismissing a parent's confusion, memory loss, or depression as a natural result of age can be an incorrect judgment. It is helpful to find a doctor interested enough in eliminating physical and organic causes before he shrugs his shoulders and gives the condition a general label. I did not do this, probably because of my father's advanced age, and my ability frequently to change his mood or outlook during visits. In addition, as a diabetic, Dad occasionally suffered lapses and metabolic changes causing confusion.

Making Financial Decisions

How thankful I was that I had insisted Dad give me the power of attorney while he and Mother were still together in their apartment. The shock of his fall, and Mother's confusion while being moved to our home, rendered both of them incapable of making financial decisions or paying bills. However, this presented a whole new area of responsibility for Bill and me. Some investments were out of state; others were earning very low interest. Dad's records were complete, but complicated. As I studied them, a sort of inflating balloon seemed to rise in my chest, a fearful foreign invader, causing me to feel dizzy and incompetent.

When I prayed about this awesome task for someone of my ability (or lack of it), the Lord assured me that He would see me through. Truly He did, opening the right doors for counseling, showing me that I could indeed be a steward of my parents' resources. Through all those years, as I filled out forms, waited in Medicare offices, transferred funds, and paid bills, the Lord gave me peace and confidence. For many the mechanics of financial transactions may be a simple task; I had much to learn. I praise God that in our case there were financial resources. For those families whose finances are extremely limited, prayer is the necessary beginning to knowing where to go for help, how to deal with other family members who may need to help, and how to seek creative options in care.

My father had been a businessman and my mother his book-keeper. They were frugal people, survivors of the Great Depression. As a child, I remember that when we vacationed by car every penny we spent was recorded. Gas was 18¢ a gallon then, and a spacious apartment rented for $30 a month. What I found to be the greatest stumbling block in my task as power of attorney was conveying to Dad the method I used to manage his finances. Financial terminology had changed as well as his ability to comprehend; inflation, interest rates, and nursing home charges bewildered him further. I was frustrated and insecure when he questioned me.

Dealing with Confusion

Darkness and confusion began to spread in Dad's mind like a cancer. Stripped of his record books, his wallet, and checkbook, he felt lost and disoriented. One day, as I came in the door, he shouted, "Am I glad to see you!" I never knew what this might portend, for it was a favorite phrase. It meant that something was troubling him, and he looked to me to solve it.

This particular visit occurred some months after Bill and I had sold one house and bought another. Dad had visited our new home in his wheelchair and had dinner with us.

"You know what I think?" he hollered, gripping the arms of the wheelchair. "That man—that man who lived on a hill—has taken my money and bought a house with it!" (Our former house was situated on a hill.)

"What man, Dad?" I asked.

"That man who bought the house!" his brow wrinkled deeply.

"Do you mean Bill?"

"Yes, yes."

Quietly I reached to take the big hand, now clenched in anger. "Bill is my husband, Daddy, and you know him very well. Now stop and think—do you believe he would take your money?"

The brow relaxed a bit. He touched his chin.

"Bill," I repeated, "your son-in-law. Do you really think he would take your money?"

A little smile played around his lips. It spread sheepishly as he began to laugh at himself. "No, no, I don't think that. I don't know what happens to me. My head gets mixed up, but you always straighten me out!"

Bringing my father face to face with the facts was a constant task. At the time I didn't give it a name, but psychologists call it *reality therapy*.

In order to help my father deal with worries about his finances,

I periodically brought him a paper listing his assets, where they were located, and the names of the banks or firms where I transacted his business. He would study them carefully, and always thank me profusely. "This has relieved my mind," he would say each time. Later he would not remember that I had brought this accounting, and I would need to do it over again. (It is important not to leave papers or statements with your parents, where they might be misplaced, read by others, or stolen.)

Being without a wallet was very disturbing to Dad. "Suppose they take up a collection here?" he asked me. "I don't have any money!" Of course large sums could not be left in his bedside table, but I brought a few quarters and put them in his drawer, for which he was very grateful. He never remembered they were there, but if he asked again, I would show them to him, and he would be satisfied. Small ways to relieve anxiety!

Even for those of us not in a confused state, Dr. Archibald D. Hart has a good word in his book *Feeling Free:*

> We depend on one another for reality. Whatever else it takes to set our *real* selves free, it can only happen in the context of our relating to one another. There is no way we can become real in isolation. We need people to make it happen. It seems to me that this is how God has ordained it, whether we like it or not. Why else would He have had so much to say about love? And forgiveness? And caring? It is only in our blending with one another that these can happen.... Place psychotics in an accepting and understanding community and they get better. Surround an alcoholic with support and caring, and he gives up his alcohol. Communities, we are discovering, can be powerful and therapeutic change agents.... Why should this loneliness and psychological isolation prevent us from

becoming real? Primarily because it prevents us from meeting our basic needs in a safe and stress-free manner. We all need to be loved, feel secure, be recognized, and have companionship—and these needs can only be met satisfactorily when we have significant "others" to whom to relate (Fleming H. Revell, p. 169).

Jesus as Your Example

You may be the *other* in the life of a now-dependent parent. When attacked unfairly by a senile parent, you need to let Christ in you reveal Himself to your parent. Jesus was real with the people He came in contact with. "Daughter, your faith has made you well" (Luke 8:48), He said to the woman with the hemorrhage. At the house of a synagogue official, He entered and said directly to the mourners, "Stop weeping, for she has not died, but is asleep" (Luke 8:52). They laughed at Him, but what did He do? He put them all out and entered the child's room, where He called her back to life.

How directly Jesus addressed the woman of Samaria when they met at the well! Not only did He lead her to confront the reality of her own life, but He told her, "I who speak to you am He [the Messiah]" (John 4:26).

We can learn from our Lord's example how to deal with those around us. By being firm and loving, we can attempt to bring a parent or friend back to the reality of the situation. Pray for dispersion of the darkness in that mind. It is tiring, and it is work, but it is the best way to help our parents and ourselves.

Perhaps an early relationship with your parent has left you without love or respect for him. If you were abused, physically or emotionally; if your parent was an alcoholic, one who neglected his family responsibility or tried to rule your affairs throughout your adulthood, your Adamic nature may want to strike out, to pay back or hurt. But if you have received new life in Christ, you must will to love that person as Christ loves, praying before each visit with the parent, asking God for the grace, forgiveness, and caring.

Some days Mother responded to my suggestion to go outside to enjoy a spring breeze and the blooming quince, or to attend a musical program in the dayroom. On other days her poor circulation and weakening heart caused sleepiness or an altered personality. For several months she frequently "saw pictures on the wall." Often portraying pleasant memories of her past, the pictures included beautiful flowers, handmade quilts, a horse and buggy; sometimes the "Muppets" or a Russian cossack dancer! Telling me about them, she appeared neither frightened nor upset—they seemed to provide entertainment. The doctor called them *senile hallucinations.*

After visiting her one day when she was particularly foggy, I returned home and wrote:

> I came to see you today, Mother
> But you weren't there.
> You feared this day, and yet,
> Now that it's come,
> Your spirit is gentle and unafraid.
>
> I came to see you today, Mother,
> But you weren't there.
> You knew me, and spoke,
> But somehow, it wasn't you.
> "I saw those pictures on the wall again," you said.
> "A man with a plow. A beautiful flower."
>
> I came to see you today, Mother
> And we really couldn't talk.

Your world was different from mine.
The man with the plow.
Is he the one Jesus talks about in Luke?
"No man, having put his hand to the plow,
And looking back, is fit for the kingdom of God."
The flower. Is it a lily of the field?

I came to see you today, Mother,
And though I wept, I won't look back.
I will look forward to your entrance
Into the kingdom.
I bent to kiss you.
"The Lord be with," I said.
"Oh, He is," you answered, and closed your eyes
For a nap.

"Is your mother dead for you?" The words dared to penetrate my own mind. Yes, as Dr. Tournier said, I no longer shared intimate confidences with my mother, for the response had changed; I no longer asked my father for his advice—now he turned to me. A certain form of death had occurred. As I observed it, I knew that, one day, it could happen to me. Now was the time to meditate upon the words of St. Paul in 2 Cor. 12:9: "My grace is sufficient for you, for power is perfected in weakness." *The Amplified Bible* reads this way:

But He said to me, "My grace—My favor and lovingkindness and mercy—are enough for you, (that is, sufficient against any danger and to enable you to bear the trouble manfully); for My strength and power are made perfect—and completed and show themselves most effective—in your weakness." Therefore, I will all the more gladly glory in my weaknesses and infirmities, that the strength and the power of Christ, the Messiah, may rest—yes, may pitch a tent (over) and dwell—upon me!

10
A Mind Set on the Spirit

"For the mind set on the flesh is death, but the mind set on the Spirit is life and peace." Romans 8:6

"I will pray the Father, and He shall give you another Comforter, that He may abide with you forever." John 14:16, KJV

"If we live by the Spirit, let us also walk in the Spirit." Galatians 5:25

The man dressed in black stood in the doorway of the church fellowship hall holding a Bible. At the opposite end of the room I was entertaining a church circle with a humorous reading in the style, I thought, of Cornelia Otis Skinner. I was 17, a member of the church, and happy to use my speaking talent to entertain those who asked me.

As I finished and the women laughed and clapped, that big Bible was raised high at the back of the hall. "Young woman!"

came the thunderous words, "you are misusing the talent God gave you! With that voice you should be reading to us from the Psalms!"

I don't remember the reaction of the women there, but I have never forgotten the admonition from that visiting missionary. Not that it made any difference in my life's direction. I went on to study radio and theater, and later television. I played roles in community theater and acted as commentator for fashion shows. My voice was used to persuade people to buy jewelry, cars, and clothes.

Many years later, when I knelt beside Ruth's bed in the nursing home and read the Psalms as she lay dying, I knew what the missionary had meant; I knew then the pain he felt the night he called out to me like an Old Testament prophet.

Responding to the Holy Spirit

In his book *Quench Not the Spirit*, Myron Augsburger wrote:

> The Spirit has come to guide us into all truth. As we study the Bible, the Spirit brings to bear on our lives new insights that will advance our spiritual growth. We are commanded to grow in grace. Many believers have a prolonged spiritual infancy because they have long quenched the Spirit in suppressing His voice. The old saying applies here, "None is so blind as one who will not see." The sin of suppressing the Spirit's insights rather than surrendering to them has robbed many a professing Christian of joy in the Lord. Some Christians after 10 or 20 years have less joy and enthusiasm than at the time of their conversion. There are many church members whom God has long sought to lead on into His fullness, who are habitually quenching the Spirit and thus robbing themselves of the fruitfulness of the abundant life.

> Quenching the Spirit is a sin marked by complacency, indifference, and being satisfied with the status quo. The Bible refers to this sin as self-righteousness, counting oneself as good enough in his present state. Such persons are closed to further revelation of God's purpose in their lives (Herald Press, Choice Books edition, p. 57).

I knew that as a professing Christian the Holy Spirit dwelt within me, but it was many years later when He convicted me of my lifestyle and I asked for the release of His power in my life. No one should feel condemned while reading this account of the Holy Spirit's work in my life. In no way do I mean to judge or criticize Christians whose occupations may be similar to mine at that time. It is not the occupation that is wrong; it is how it fits into God's plan for one's life. God works differently in each of us. Each is a unique creation, able to respond and act in different ways.

Since I grew up in a Bible-oriented church whose ministers preached from the Word, I was without excuse but not until the 60s, when widespread teaching of the Person and work of the Holy Spirit reached the corner where Bill and I were planted, did we know something was missing in our lives. The enabling power of the Holy Spirit came at a time when life's tragedies made a painful mosaic of our days. God knew our need, and His timing was perfect.

As we grow older and as we interact with aged parents and other relatives, the work of the Holy Spirit builds a foundation for grace and wisdom in these relationships.

The late Catherine Marshall in her book *The Helper* (Guideposts, p. 32), listed what the Holy Spirit gives us:

Personal awareness of God's love	The fruit of the Spirit
Conviction of who Christ is	Joy
A message of help to others	Renewal
The right words to speak in times of stress	Guidance from God
Comprehension of the thoughts and mind of God	Healing (except what nature or doctors can give us)
Help in our weaknesses	The ability to set our minds on things of the Spirit
Freedom from slavery to sin and harmful habits	An Intercessor with the Father
Any of the gifts of the Spirit	The pledge of eternal life

Years before the time when I asked the Spirit to control my life, He was in control as part of the Trinity without my acknowledgment. Looking back, I know His guidance and protection were present without my knowledge—which makes God's love even more precious!

Now that we have seven grandchildren, I am aware of how young we can be to grasp God's truth. When I was a child, our church traditionally gave its seven-year-olds Bibles. Before we received them, our minister told us a story: he had visited a parishioner's home, and when he asked for their Bible, it was removed from a bookshelf and *dusted*. Actually, he showed us how the lady blew the dust off the book! "I never want to come to *your* home," he said, "and find that *your* Bible is dusty." I never forgot that, and it was probably the reason I began to read that Bible every night when I was 11. Later, I would understand Jesus' words: "The worry of the world, and the deceitfulness of riches choke the Word, and it becomes unfruitful" (Matt. 13:22).

Walking in the Spirit

When we belong to the Lord, are filled with the Spirit, and live in the Spirit, the Bible says we should also walk in the Spirit. To me this means that my steps are "ordered by the Lord" and as I submit to Him and to my understanding of His Word and His guidance through prayer, I can step out in faith and trust Him to accomplish His plan.

To honor our parents without feeling guilt over our relationship with them is not only possible, it is healthy and desirable. The Holy Spirit will give us the qualities we need to establish this kind of decisiveness—the ability to forgive, to order priorities, to assess and care for true needs. By comparing our qualities with the fruit of the Spirit (Gal. 5:22), we know whether we are walking in the Spirit. However, if we see ourselves lacking this fruit there is no reason to condemn ourselves. Christ died for the ungodly, and we stand clean before the Father, as Jesus intercedes for us. When we meditate on that fact it truly produces joy.

The Holy Spirit guides us in different ways: He protects us, He gives us wisdom, and He moves us into God's plan for our lives with His power.

Several years ago, I was driving home at dusk with three ministers who had gone to a meeting opposing the building of an abortion center in a nearby city. As I rounded a sharp turn, a voice called in my ear, "Slow down! Slow down!" Obediently

I put my foot on the brake, throwing my passengers forward; but as we rounded the turn, there, directly in front of us, was a farm tractor inching along without lights. Traveling at normal speed, we would have crashed into the vehicle. No one else heard the voice, but if I had dismissed or ignored it, disaster would have resulted.

How often we have said, "I don't know what to do." And we don't. At the time I had to decide whether or not to move my mother from our home to Medical Care Center, the Spirit provided wisdom.

We all have those times when we ask, "Is it my own flesh, my own desires? Is it Satan trying to influence me?" Not easy, is it? But we are not dependent on ourselves. Sometimes as we ask His guidance, He simply answers, *wait*. I know in my spirit when I hear that word. I prefer not to hear it, but when I obey and wait He provides the answer at the right time, and I am spared the entanglements and string pulling that we humans do to effect what we think is the answer to our question. Sometimes the answer is *act!* It truly helps to have a spouse or prayer partner confirm what we have heard from the Lord.

God knew that Bill and I desired to know Him in a deeper way. I believe that is why we got our unmistakable marching orders to go to the Holy Land. In 1978 we were part of a fellowship group, some of whom were planning to go on a trip sponsored by the New Directions Evangelistic Association of Burlington, North Carolina. At that time both my parents were residents of the nursing home. As an only child, I had repeatedly stated that I would never leave the country while my parents were living. One night at the dinner table Bill and I were discussing the trip which would include Egypt and Jordan, as well as Israel.

Suddenly in the midst of our discussion we looked up at each other, forks in mid air. "Why, we're talking as though we are going, aren't we!" We were astonished. Someone else had made that decision for us. And truly, He had. A mountaintop experience, the trip added an incomparable spiritual depth and luster to our lives. For many reasons, we see now that if we had not recognized the Holy Spirit's guidance at that time, we would probably never have made that trip. Every door was opened for us. I never had a fear or moment of hesitation when we planned the trip or while we were away. His peace came as we followed God's direction and operated in His will.

The Guidance of the Holy Spirit
Two weeks and three days after our return from Israel, my father died. Yes, we had gone in God's timing.

We can make good decisions on our own by assessing various possibilities and weighing alternatives. Excellent secular books are available on a wide variety of subjects designed to change our lifestyles and help us become more mature and able to make sensible and realistic decisions and choices, but as Christians we learn to rely ultimately on the guidance of the Holy Spirit, which is far superior to human wisdom. By reading Scripture with a listening ear and an open heart, by using the mind God has given us, and in some cases receiving a confirming word from another, we can exercise our God-given "uncommon" sense in decision making. Sometimes, of course, we do not make good decisions in spite of trying to do as God directs. Everything we do does not turn out perfectly, but we can trust that God's hand is in it (Rom. 8:28).

Some of us act rashly according to immediate needs and should recognize that trait in ourselves by slowing down and asking God to step in. Others have the opposite problem—not being able to make decisions. If this is a regular occurrence, we need to get to the root of our inability to make decisions. Sometimes this requires professional help, but for most of us, sorting out priorities is the answer. Even though one particular aspect may seem urgent, it is not always the important one. If Christ has set us free, we should be free from what others think (that is, free to be ourselves in Christ, though others may not agree with our decisions). If we aren't, frustration will set in and bind us with its aggravating cords.

Relief from Stress
Because of stress from the uncertain economy and current lifestyles, the world offers various means of relaxation such as yoga, Eastern meditation, hypnosis, and astrology. As Christians, we know that none of these constitutes a favorable answer. Some actually bring people to mental breakdown, demon possession, or at the very least, false hopes. Christian meditation, however, focused on Scripture, brings life and peace.

We need to know God. But the wonderful part is that He knows us, and as we seek Him, He shows us how to deal with stress. Over and over in the Bible we are told to ask, to seek, to knock. Instead, we flounder around like a tired swimmer who has gone out too far.

While my parents were in the nursing home, I was able to appropriate short times of rest and relaxation. Sometimes before visiting, I would sit for 10 minutes in the lobby, eyes closed, consciously relaxing muscles tensed by working and driving. Other times, while Mother sat in her recliner and Dad in his wheelchair, I stretched out on the bed, removed my shoes and read my mail. If you think you are not free enough to behave this way, try it anyway! You may find that a relaxed presence can often do much for a parent, while giving you time to rest, and allowing you the opportunity to assess the general routine of care.

On several occasions one parent was hospitalized while the other remained in the nursing home, and I needed to visit two places. Because I am able to doze quickly and be refreshed (truly a gift from God!) I would park my car and rest my arms and head on the steering wheel, drifting and dozing, unwinding the tenseness of the body and the whirling of my mind. Then the Spirit could minister to me, much the same way Elijah was refreshed under the juniper tree. Doing this before each visit kept me in one piece.

These ways may not be helpful to everyone. Maybe you'd rather park a distance away from the hospital (as I did occasionally) and relax by walking briskly between car and hospital. Doing stretching exercises, or reading something totally new may be relaxing. Listening to tapes in the car may pave the way for a visit. Whatever the choice, do it! Work it into the time frame of your lifestyle.

Almost two years after Dad's death, I reached a plateau of distress. Mother and I both needed a change beyond our brief time outside on the patio. The sameness of her room, the meals, the tedium of existence threatened to overwhelm both of us. Our relationship was deteriorating due to the state of her physical and mental health and my weariness. Then, true to my impulsive nature, I decided to look at another nursing home, more costly, but newer and different, with changes I felt would be beneficial to both of us. I toured, I talked, I listened, I counseled with my husband. Then I sat to pray. I made the decision to move Mother, even knowing the change might confuse her further.

The very next day, when I began the necessary paper work, my mother suffered a massive stroke. She was never moved. She remained in the same bed, with the people who knew her best caring for her. Five weeks later she died.

I am convinced that when we walk in the Spirit to the extent that we understand and grasp that walk, God honors our individual personalities, answering according to our needs and His will through His bountiful mercy and wisdom.

11
A Heart May Be Happy

"A good name is better than good ointment, and the day of one's death is better than the day of one's birth. It is better to go to a house of mourning, than to go to a house of feasting, because that is the end of every man, and the living takes it to heart. Sorrow is better than laughter, for when a face is sad, a heart may be happy."
Ecclesiastes 7:1-3

Death's shadow came suddenly in my paternal grandparents' home. At age 89, Grandpa had been bedridden only a few days. Twelve hours before he died, Grandma's stroke took her quickly. I recall the community's astonishment at the deaths of the couple only a few hours apart. There was a double funeral, which I recall, though I was only 7.

Most of our great-grandparents and even grandparents died in their own homes—nursed, bathed, and fed by a succession of relatives from the large families who lived nearby. Today oxygen tanks, tubes, catheters, and respirators are used in the green-toned corridors of mercy where most people die.

In addition to contending with the grief, and perhaps anger and guilt, at the time of a parent's death today, often we must decide whether we will permit plastic and steel to sustain or comfort aged people at the doorway of death. Our minds are confused by the accounts of euthanasia, and with such phrases as *death with dignity,* and *quality of expected life.* We question distinctions between ordinary and extraordinary means of sustaining life, for we view life as a gift and a trust.

Professor Paul Ramsey wrote:

> Why not say that the classification *ordinary/ extraordinary* can simply be reduced to 1) a determination either of the treatment indicated or that there is no treatment indicated in the case of the dying and 2) a patient's right to refuse treatment? The answer to that question is that there are medically indicated treatments (these used to be called ordinary) that a competent conscious patient has no moral right to refuse, just as no one has a moral right to deliberately ruin his health. Treatment refusal is a relative right, contrary to what is believed today by those who would reduce medical ethics to patient autonomy and a "right to die." In this connection we need to recall that the reasons alleged to warrant refusal or extraordinary treatments were worked out in times that were medically primitive. Because of progress in medical practice, more and more extraordinary treatments have today become ordinary. These are surely medically indicated and desirable (*Ethics at the Edges of Life,* Yale University Press, p. 156).

Sorting It Out

Medically and legally I have no expertise in making these decisions. I have tried to understand these ethics in terms of the familiar: my parents and others I have observed. My father lived to be 94 only because he had daily injections of insulin; occasionally he suffered insulin shock, requiring emergency care. Today the diabetic's treatments are *ordinary* and to refuse my father his insulin dose, whatever his age or condition of health, would be morally offensive. In contrast, I learned of a 96-year-old lady taken to the emergency room of a hospital in heart failure. Employing CPR (cardiopulmonary resuscitation) caused her several broken ribs, and a few weeks of increased suffering before death. I see no reason why a lady of that age should not be allowed to die of heart failure without the resuscitative means available today.

In his book, *Let the Patient Decide,* Louis Shattuck Baer, M.D. wrote:

> As a family doctor, I have often found that the greatest social pressures on me to continue existence-sustaining measures in a patient come from a patient's family. When an emergency medical problem, such as a severe stroke in a previously healthy patient, suddenly confronts the grown children, they will insist that "everything possible be done" for their mother or that "the finest specialist" be called in to save their father.
>
> Any hint from the doctor that it might be better to relax and let matters take their course is not well received unless such a possibility has been carefully discussed by the patient and the family before it occurs. That does not take place as often as it should. It is the exception, not the rule.
>
> With the hundredfold increase in the ability of medical science to prolong biologic existence, frequently by very simple measures, adult children have to learn to let their parents go. A wife or husband must now learn to help the mate, by doing *less* medically rather than by doing *more.*

When some member over 65 can no longer communicate and is confronted by the possibility of years of total invalidism and dependence, too few families consider carefully enough the circumstances. So the doctor is asked: Is there a chance he will live? Will she speak? The chance may be less than one in a thousand, but the family clings to it. The intravenous with its antibiotics drips on, and a death from natural causes (a stroke, for example) that would have come quickly in three to five days with just good nursing care is *transformed into three years in a nursing home,* by the well-intentioned, simple but so effective medical measures that have been used.

The dilemma is difficult in the extreme for the doctor and the family. But it won't fade away. It must be discussed widely by all older citizens. If more people discuss this problem well in advance, doctors and families can find a better approach than we have so far. For the next of kin of a stuporous or comatose patient to say, "Do everything you can and if that fails I pray the Lord will take him," or "I can't play God," may well lead away from *life* and ensure years of *nonliving* in a nursing home for the patient (The Westminister Press, pp. 39-40).

I can agree with much of what Dr. Baer suggests in his book, but not all. He does not advocate mercy killing or direct euthanasia at any time; however, his references to the First Euthanasia Conference of November 23, 1968 as well as quotes from the publication *Euthanasia,* the Hindu scriptures, and the Yan and Ying of Taoism leave me uneasy as an evangelical Christian.

Defining Active Euthanasia
Dr. Joseph Fletcher, an ordained Episcopal clergyman and visiting professor of Medical Ethics at the University of Virginia, Charlottesville, authored *Situation Ethics; A New Morality*

(Westminister Press, 1966). When I heard Dr. Fletcher speak on euthanasia at Virginia's Hampden-Sydney College in 1974 he discussed the Bible, Jesus' teachings, and his own philosophical reasonings, yet he is a signer of the *Humanist Manifesto II* which declares, "Faith in a prayer-hearing God assumed to love and care for persons, to hear and understand their prayers, and to be able to do something about them, is an unproved and outmoded faith. . . . No deity will save us; we must save ourselves" (The American Humanist Association).

When I asked him publicly how he could reconcile his ordination as an Episcopal clergyman with his signing of the *Humanist Manifesto,* he had no concrete answer. He is outspoken in his argument for the "dignity of dying" through *active* enthanasia! He begins his argument by writing:

> What follows is a moral defense of euthanasia. Primarily, I mean active or positive enthanasia, which helps the patient to die; not merely the passive or negative form of euthanasia, which "lets the patient go" by simply withholding life-preserving treatment ("Ethics and Euthanasia," *To Live and To Die,* Robert H. Williams, Editor, Springer-Verlag, p. 113).

Evil often creeps in where good is intended. That too is the danger of *legislating* "death with dignity."

> "Active enthanasia," says Father Paul Marx, O. S. B., "entails a direct intervention, a direct killing of a person with or without his knowledge or consent. It is the administration of a lethal dose or the deliberate refusal to use even the ordinary means of preserving life. Passive euthanasia is merely the avoidance or discontinuation of

extraordinary means of preserving life. It usually refers to removing supportive equipment or drug treatment when a patient has irrevocably entered the process of dying" (Catherine M. Anthony, "The 'Right to Die,'" *Our Sunday Visitor*, Feb. 24, 1980).

In a pastoral letter that he wrote in 1975, Bishop Walter F. Sullivan of the Catholic Diocese of Richmond, Virginia stated:

The delicate relationships of a dying person with his or her family, doctor and minister are very fragile and vary from case to case. Each case must be treated with the individual care that the individual's dignity demands. It is certainly not desirable to create legislation which will ultimately deny any individual that dignity, and at the same time, destroy those personal relationships. . . . [By specifying in law] we make the doctor himself an agent of society and of the law rather than an advocate of life and the patient. It is indeed quite possible that the pressure of the law and the fear of legal suit or indictment of homicide will force the doctor to maintain extraordinary life-support systems in the absence of the "living will." If there is indeed genuine fear of malpractice suits, then the issue to be addressed is malpractice legislation, not "death with dignity" legislation ("Death With Dignity: Ministry, Not Legislation," a pastoral letter).

This is a complicated issue which we cannot discuss at length here, except to say that there are medically indicated procedures or reasonable therapy to *ease* rather than *prolong* life for the terminally ill or the voiceless dying aged.

Assessing Methods of Care

An understanding relationship with your parent's doctor is important if your parent is extremely ill. If you are one of several children scattered around the country, you may get phone calls that ask: "What does the doctor say?" If it is possible, establish good communication with the physician before the time comes when you have to make decisions concerning the type and amount of medical interference you and the doctor will allow. Know what shapes the doctor's ethics and his feelings concerning geriatric patients. When a parent is moved so that he may live with you or near you, it is sometimes difficult to find the kind of physician you would like. At least know how he responds to geriatric illnesses.

A question you may ask yourself that will help you and the doctor assess the method of care for your parent at time of extreme illness is, *Am I, by this action, prolonging the process of dying, or am I, by this technology, preserving life?*

The concept of the hospice has been increasingly employed as a means to minister to the dying. In addition to painkillers and good nursing care, an important aspect is the setting in which the dying person can be heard, understood, and loved. This compassionate approach may be adopted by you and other caregivers during the dying process of your loved one.

The hospice program has expanded rapidly in the last few years, providing a way for terminally ill patients to live with as little pain as possible, and more peace and emotional comfort. More than 800 hospice programs exist throughout the country. The emphasis is on keeping the patient at home, with family, friends, and visiting professionals involved in care. Though the majority of patients are suffering from cancer, many are elderly patients with a variety of disorders. Some hospice programs are hospital-based units; others are in nursing homes or in separate facilities. New insurance coverage (federal and private), as well as other aspects of hospice, make this an attractive option to provide the terminally ill with more comfort.

Love, not guilt, should be the motivating force when you walk through those dark valleys. Hopefully there is time in your life, even now perhaps, to forgive your parent and forgive yourself for the hurts of the past, and to be honest before God that He may cleanse you from fear, and even hatred. Forgiving brothers and sisters is important, too, for resentment and anger toward siblings often surfaces at the time of a parent's serious illness. "Forgive us our debts, as we forgive our debtors" (Matt. 6:12) needs to be a way of life.

During the last few months of Dad's life, he often would position his wheelchair at the entrance of his room, looking for me. When I walked toward him, his face would exhibit confusion, fear, and even desperation. The nurses' reports were bad. He did not know where he was. He kicked them while they dressed the unyielding ulcer on his leg or administered insulin. He spit out his medication. His pills were crushed and mixed with applesauce, and a male orderly helped during treatment times. He no longer read a newspaper or talked about the cars outside his window.

He was sure no one was paying his bills. "We can't afford this motel!" he shouted, distressing Mother.

One day when I arrived, I spotted his chair down the hall. "This contraption just won't go! And I put gas in it! Give me some money!" he yelled, inching his way past room doors.

"Where are you going?" I asked, facing him.

"To Ilion. I have to deliver these flowers."

His mind had regressed to his occupation of an earlier time in his life. It was harder to bring him back to the present, to indicate to him that his wheelchair was not a truck or a car.

Words escaped him. An ambulance was a "hurry-up wagon." Pushing him back to his room did not help. He was hyperactive and agitated, occasionally requiring sedation at night.

Between Life and Death

Then came the day of God's grace, soon after our return from the trip to Israel. Dad was quieter that day, pensive, eyelids fluttering as he sat by the window. Suddenly he brightened.

"I can see it!" he called out happily. "There are special rooms for children!"

Thinking he was referring to the parochial school in sight of his room, I answered, "Oh, the school over there."

"No! No!" he insisted. "There's a place for everyone, but you can't enter on the ground floor!"

The spirit suddenly illuminated my heart. "Dad," I asked, "do you mean the place where Jesus said 'In My house are many mansions and I have prepared a place for you?'"

"Yes, that's it!" He was joyful.

Malcolm Muggeridge, author, lecturer, novelist, says it this way:

> When you're old, as I am, there are all sorts of extremely pleasant things that happen to you. For one, you realize that history is nonsense. But the pleasantest thing of all is that you wake up in the night and you find that you are half in and half out of your battered old carcass. It seems quite a toss-up whether you go back and resume full occupancy of your mortal body, or make off toward the bright glow you see in the sky, the lights of the city of God. In this limbo between life and death, you know beyond any shadow of doubt that, as an infinitesimal particle of God's creation, you are a participant in God's purpose for His creation, and that that purpose is loving and not hating, is

creative and not destructive, is everlasting and not tempo-
ral, is universal and not particular. With this certainty
comes an extraordinary sense of comfort and joy ("Human
Utopia: The Great Liberal Death Wish," *Christianity Today,*
Sept. 3, 1982, p. 42).

A few minutes after his vision of the rooms, Dad dozed off,
his forehead peaceful, lips relaxed, gnarled hands folded over
his patchwork lap robe.

During the next few days a dark terror again seized my
father. The sunlight from heaven disappeared behind the clouds
of darkness as Dad argued, fought, and insulted everyone, causing Mother to retreat into sullenness and sleep. I asked our
daughter Claire if she could agree to pray with me for Dad's
release in death. She said she could. Three days after our
agreement, the nursing home held a Memorial Day picnic complete with hot dogs, hamburgers, and balloons. The cooks wore
gala aprons and hats. As I helped the patients on the warm,
breezy patio, a nurse pushed my father's chair toward me.
Within a few minutes, after refusing all food, he became ill and
was rushed back to his room. Two days later, at 7:30 in the
morning, the doctor telephoned. "Your father has just died," he
told me.

"Praise the Lord," I said evenly.

"Yes," said the doctor.

Two funeral services were scheduled: one in Lynchburg, for
the benefit of my mother, and another in Utica where he was
buried. During the service I shared the story of Dad's vision of
the rooms. My face was sad, but my heart was indeed happy,
for my confused father had entered that specially prepared
place, and God had been gracious enough to let me know it.

A year and a half later Mother suffered a severe "cardiovascular accident," and entered the process of dying. Paul Ramsey's book, *Ethics at the Edges of Life,* asks the question:

> How can the *process of dying* be identified? How do you know that an infant or a comatose patient is dying? I do not. The reply must be that this is a *medical* judgment and that physicians can and do determine—in human, no doubt fallible judgment—the difference between dying and nondying terminal patients. In the case of those whose death is impending, further attempted salvic treatment can only prolong dying. In the case of nondying terminal patients, however, care calls for making treatment available to sustain them even when this only improves their condition or adds meager life to their days. Both the dying and the incurable if conscious and competent have, in addition, a right to refuse treatment or, better said, to participate in the choice of their treatment (including the choice of no further attempted cures) (Yale, p. 187).

If a parent is in this dying process (whether he is 50 or 90), honoring him means employing biblical ethics bathed in the purest kind of love. This is no small order. This kind of love should be the caring love of Jesus. If we have worked through our forgiveness, been relieved of our guilt, and cast our burdens on the Lord, we are ready to live day by day, moment by moment.

The Dying Process

Much of the real suffering that goes on during the dying process of a loved one is ours, not the patient's. As a parent nears the entrance to the city of God, we view "the battered old carcass." It may seem that the spirit has almost slipped from the body, leaving a shell. The spirit may be anxious to leave, but those very organs that were formed in the first few weeks after conception are still working to preserve life.

The ordinary treatment for my mother included pureed foods and liquid administered orally with a feeding syringe (usually by Bertha, who took all the time needed and talked gently to Mother as she fed her). Nearby, like a soldier on guard duty, stood an oxygen tank for those times when her breathing became labored. She was turned in her bed every two hours to change position. After two weeks, the doctor ordered a catheter. All of these procedures provided sustenance and as much physical comfort as possible. As the days stretched out, Mother was able to receive less food and liquid; Bertha documented the intake.

"Look," a young aide said to me, "her skin isn't resilent." She pinched up some skin on her patient's arm. "She's dehydrating. She needs an IV."

Though the doctor did not suggest or encourage this, I knew I could insist on intravenous feeding. This would not bring life back to Mother's eyes or mind; it would not restore movement to paralyzed limbs, it would prolong the dying process. As long as Mother could still take liquids by mouth, I decided I was free to refuse an IV, especially when it was not indicated by the physician.

Communicate Love

More important at this time, I felt, was communication and touch. I held the hand unaffected by the stroke and asked her questions, requesting that she squeeze my hand. There was no response. One day, I stroked her face and told her I thought she could hear me. "I know this must be so hard—not to be able to answer me. I want you to know I think you can hear me. Can you?"

Slowly her lips formed one slurred word: "Sure!"

"Thank You, Lord!" I called out. I was encouraged then to sing one of her favorite hymns, "Love Divine, All Loves Excelling." Her eyes usually remained closed; when open, they appeared unseeing, but I knew then that she could hear, be encouraged, and prayed for aloud! She was not imprisoned in an impenetrable darkness; the Word of Life could be administered along with oxygen, living water along with apple juice!

When a Christmas arrangement of her favorite carnations arrived from her sisters, I held it close to her, telling her who had sent it and what it looked like. I never treated her as though she were absent, comatose, or under anesthesia. One of the greatest mistakes doctors, nurses, and family make, in my opinion, is to discuss the patient's condition in her presence.

Part of my suffering during this time were the wrenching changes. My emotions were stretched to accept death, then stretched to accept life again. Three times a call came from the nursing home that death was imminent: her eyes were fixed, her breathing unduly labored, her color changed. I rushed off, only to find Mother rallying, holding on to the last thread of life she had loved so much. Bertha told me Mother had incredible tenacity. As she lingered, appearing to be in a place of suffering, I finally bent over her and whispered, "Dear, can you just let go? Can you let go to Him?" Whether or not she heard me, I don't know; but two days later, she did let go, into the arms of her Saviour.

"Casting all your anxiety on Him, because He cares for you" (1 Peter 5:7). Let us rejoice and not weep, for death is a part of life, controlled by our heavenly Father. We are upheld by His omnipotent hand. It is time for praise and worship, to prepare ourselves for the meeting at the Throne.

12
What Does the Lord Require?

"He has told you, O man, what is good; and what does the Lord require of you but to do justice, to love kindness, and to walk humbly with your God?" Micah 6:8

I have often thought of the truth of the doctor's words, "You can provide for your mother's comfort, but not for her happiness." Whether a parent assumes any responsibility for his or her own happiness, under new conditions in her life, is another story.

Usually it is our parents' comfort and safety that we are concerned about first. We see these old people, now our responsibility, faltering. They have an auto accident that is their fault; they consistently leave the stove burner on and forget their medications; their dishes and clothes are not washed clean, or they skimp on meals. Memory losses intensify; handling money is a mountainous chore.

"How can Mom be *safe* in that house? The neighborhood is going downhill—two old people were robbed last week!"

"How can Dad make it through the winter? He turns the heat down so low I'm afraid he'll freeze!"

"Mom's eyesight is getting so bad she took the wrong pills yesterday!"

We feel the need to provide for parents whose comfort and safety are in jeopardy. Should something devastating occur, we would feel responsible and guilty that we had not acted sooner. And so, when we see these changes in the lives of a parent or parents, we know that something must be done to protect them from possible harm, and to relieve our consciences.

The Beginning of Change

When an incident occurs suddenly, such as a fractured hip, there is not time to think through options. If you are the nearest child, you will probably take charge, moving your parent to a hospital, and notifying other brothers or sisters after the fact.

Perhaps, though, the change is more subtle. Mary, for example, calls her mother from hundreds of miles away, and finds her unable to hear or respond coherently over the phone. She calls her brother Tom, who lives 10 miles from Mother. He too has noticed changes in Mother, and the discussion begins.

Siblings may disagree as to what is the best solution, sometimes basing their decisions on their own emotional or financial needs, rather than determining the most feasible solution in the light of the parent's real needs. In the community there may be choices which will keep that parent in her home: cleaning help, a visiting nurse, Meals-on-Wheels, regular home health care. The local Commission on Aging, the Mental Health Association, Family Service Agency, Human Services Department, or a pastor, usually know what services are available locally. These vary from state to state, from urban to rural community, but current awareness of the problems of the elderly has spawned some kind of help in nearly every area.

An extensive article in *Newsweek* (Nov. 1, 1982) examined several options when a time for change occurs. Some are unique to particular areas, such as Boston's Shared Living House, a multi-generation commune founded a few years ago by the Back Bay Aging Concerns Committee. Because ages range from 23 to the mid-80s, the occupants are not isolated from intergenerational living. Some communities have foster family programs, and matchups with housemates or tenants through such agencies as Homesharing for Seniors. Day care centers in some areas offer part-time supervision for even the severely impaired, giving relatives a chance to catch up with work or rest. About 800 such centers exist in the U.S. Many cities are now investigating homecare alternatives to nursing home confinement. Budget cuts have troubled some waters, but in other cases innovative ideas have surfaced at lower cost.

Both state and federal agencies are starting to show more sensitivity to the elderly and their families. In Georgia a new state law requires that elderly patients receive full assessment by a doctor, nurse, and social worker before admission to a nursing home, to determine what alternatives might work. Maryland is experimenting with a direct $2000 a year grant to 60 families who take care of disabled old people at home, and Congress has several bills on the agenda.

Even in largely rural areas, there are new solutions. Near Adams, New York, a small community close to the Canadian border, a middle-aged couple run a boardinghouse for 8 to 10 elderly or handicapped people. They all enjoy country cooking around a large table in the farm kitchen; a comfortable sitting room, plus their own bedrooms with their own furniture; a caring atmosphere where medications and baths are supervised. I visited this farmhouse where a mentally handicapped uncle had settled in. Among the boarders were an aged mother and her middle-aged Down's syndrome daughter. The soothing atmosphere that combined the smell of good food, comfortable chairs, television, pets, and above all, the cheerfulness of its owners, opened my eyes to the possibilities of special care for those facing "in-between places" in life. It takes gifted, energetic people with a love for the less fortunate to provide such care. The cost was far less than a nursing home.

It is well to avoid extreme changes before they are necessary. When change in a parent is gradual, by all means seek the available agencies in that community that provide help to the parent in his or her own home or apartment. Take the next step when it becomes necessary.

If for example, Meals-On-Wheels or a home health care aide can meet an immediate need, try it, though your parent may not appreciate your decision. There may be great resistance to a stranger coming into the home to bring meals, give baths, or clean house. Your parent may say, "But *you* could do this for me." The elderly parent does not always remember that the son or daughter has a full-time job, teenagers at home, poor health, or a combination of all three! I sometimes found that appealing to my parents' love for me helped a great deal. "This would be such a relief to *me*. Would you just try it?" Other times real firmness is needed as you explain the other option might be leaving their home.

If no child lives near the parent who is failing, an information and referral service in the community may be able to provide names of organizations that can help. If your parent is reluctant to call, you may need to make the contact and see what measures can be taken.

Making Decisions

As a Christian, your relationship with the Lord will greatly help you in your decisions. Spend enough time with Him alone to hear what He is saying. If you are married, consult with your spouse; if you are in the habit of praying together, this is a strengthening factor in decision-making. Some praying spouses agree to pray separately for a few days; then they come together to share what they have heard. If the answer is the same, they move ahead with confidence. If not, they talk it over, write down options, and pray again.

Probably no aspect concerning parental care in the later years is as devastating and widespread as money decisions. In their book, *You and Your Aging Parent,* Barbara Silverstone and Helen Kandel Hyman wrote:

> Money and material possessions—the abundance as well as the lack of both—very often provide the real underlying source of family dissension. Brothers and sisters have been competing over inheritances since the beginning of time. They are still doing it today, especially when their elderly parents have sizable estates to leave behind. But even when there is little money and only a few material possessions, these can still assume great symbolic worth. The struggle to win them may be out of all proportion to their value. "Mother's leaving me the silver candlesticks because I'm the oldest," or "I should get the candlesticks because I've done the most for Mother." "Doing" for Mother therefore is expected to pay off. But will this kind of "doing" really pay off for her?
>
> Money can cause trouble when there is none. If Mother is barely scraping along on her small pension and Social Security checks, and her children are in a better financial position, who is going to contribute and how much? Should

they all contribute equal amounts? Or should the contributions be from each child according to his (or her) financial situation? Or each child according to his emotional need? Will the contribution be given out of generosity or guilt? Will the gifts have strings attached? Will Mother have to subordinate her own wishes to the wishes of the biggest checkbook?

Money is therefore power: "I give Mother the most, therefore I have the right to decide what plans we should make for her." Does money ever buy that right? Many brothers and sisters say no.

Money can also be a substitute. A son who says, "I send my father a monthly check," may feel he has thereby discharged his total filial responsibility. Does his monthly check balance out equally with the brother's weekly visit or his sister's daily phone call? They may feel that their contributions have greater value, and no amount of money is a substitute for care and concern. Finally, money can become a contest. Competitive brothers and sisters who have money themselves may lavish luxuries on their elderly mother or father, not because either parent needs these gifts or even wants them, but to demonstrate which child has achieved the greatest worldly success (Pantheon Books, pp. 51-52).

If the change in your parent's condition requires the help of someone else to handle finances, you should consult a lawyer or legal aid service. If your father trusts you or a sibling enough (trust sometimes turns into suspicion in old age) to grant power of attorney, it may save you a painful court procedure at a later date. Such legal rights vary from state to state and are best determined by the caretaker in cooperation with a lawyer. A pastor or social worker may be needed to help with the change of "power."

When a child does not exercise power of attorney soon enough, a mentally incompetent parent may be bilked by unscrupulous people, write checks for services never rendered, or give away family heirlooms as payment for running errands or mowing the lawn. Firmness along with love and consistency are needed to deal with a parent whose body and mind are functioning poorly.

Love and Common Sense

Making decisions about family possessions is a touchy area for all concerned. You might encourage your parent to give away some things that would be appropriate for family weddings or graduations (with your assistance). Approach the matter of sorting and giving *some* things away in a spirit of love and common sense. Wouldn't *she* rather be the one to decide on dispersement rather than have others sorting her things? Many old people cannot resign themselves to the fact that change will occur—for all of us. Siblings (of your parent and yourself) might be called together to make some of these decisions but no matter what you do or decide in the division of material possessions you may be criticized.

Parents who are failing physically or mentally see themselves as losing control of their lives. Role reversal shakes both generations. Communication breakdowns are common, at a time when decisions on help, finances, or moves must be made. Complaints, attacks, and recrimination often occur. As a result, either nothing is accomplished or decisions are made in haste and anger. Real communication requires willingness to listen to one another.

Intermediaries often help. As in the case of my father's driving, his doctor's advice was heeded when mine was ignored. Bring in a pastor, social worker, attorney, physician, or trusted friend when you are at an impasse.

When making money decisions, be sure you have up-to-date information. Under today's constantly changing laws and regulations, both in banking and old age benefits, we need to keep current. If you do not know your parent's eligibility or entitlements under Social Security, the first step is to visit the local Social Security office. Gather whatever pertinent papers you might need from your parent; assess his assets (home ownership, automobile, savings, insurance, Medicare). Sometimes what a parent *thinks* he has coming is not correct.

Knowing What Benefits Are Available

Many people confuse Medicare, Medicaid, and Supplemental Security Income. They do not know what is covered in the event of hospitalization or nursing home admittance. Benefits are not automatic; you have to apply. The local Social Security office can give you the information you need. As you gather these facts, you are helping not only your parent, but also yourself—getting a glimpse of what you need to know about your own preparedness for old age.

The spectre of a failing Social Security system has raised specific questions in the minds of many Christians. In a thought-provoking letter to the editor, Richard E. Knodel, Jr., pastor of Grace Presbyterian church in Lynchburg, Virginia, wrote:

> The crisis over Social Security is related to biblical truth. Folks are finally admitting the crisis part. While the elderly cry out today, Paul Harvey recently noted that the young shall soon be shackled with tax increases of over 50 percent—just for Social Security!
>
> What is the Bible's position? It teaches that the family is the basic unit of life. It is the pattern for society. It was created and therefore sanctioned by God. It has certain God-given prerogatives and responsibilities.

While one is primarily responsible for his immediate family, one is also primarily responsible for his parents. In Christian circles, "If anyone does not provide for his own, and especially for those of his household he has denied the faith" (1 Tim. 5:8). Under this system, care of the elderly is a miniscule burden.

But how about today? Men snicker at the wisdom of God. They alter and revise truth at every turn. They attack family values and family inheritance and substitute novel systems. The creation family is identified as one of those anachronisms we must evolve beyond.

The bottom line is that people cry out day and night for freedom, yet pitifully vote for slavery in the humanistic choices they make. Necessity beckons us to return to biblical moorings—before our curse increases! (*The News*, Lynchburg, Va., Dec. 2, 1982)

It is true that in our society the family has undergone gross changes. Since the January 1973 Supreme Court decision for abortion on demand, over 12 million unborn babies have been aborted. Increased divorce and remarriage causes extraordinary family complications; lifestyles include homosexual "families." We are suffering a curse of our own making.

I do not believe, however, that we need to withdraw from the world and refuse to accept remuneration which is due our aged families, who worked hard and long in the expectation that they would have some measure of financial security in their later years. Rev. Knodel's letter points out the necessity of employing biblical values whenever we deal with the crucial turning points of our earthly existence. In biblical times there were no coronary bypasses or pacemakers; no antibiotics or injections; no respirators or kidney machines—certainly no man-made hearts! Those who lived long lives were able to live with minimal help—then they died.

What makes the care and the death of aged parents today (and those not aged) so complicated is the rapid growth of medical technology and availability of life-support systems that not only keep the body alive, but place excessive financial burdens on the patient, the family, and the state. Do not misunderstand that statement! Every patient deserves loving care and the use of medically approved measures to sustain life. But who is to decide who should live and who should die? We are at a dangerous crossroads in our society. Genetic engineering and experimentation provide both threat and promise. Decisions will only be as proper and ethical as those who are in control; therefore, keeping deathbed decisions within the circle of patient, doctor, and family is crucial.

Dr. Henry B. Larzelere, a physician friend, told me:

> If you as a doctor are sincere with the family and the patient, the right decision will be made. The atheistic doctors are the ones with the worst problem making a decision. They try to "play God"—try to assume that big role, saying "I'll have trouble," meaning they worry about themselves. They want laws so they may operate inside a little protective cage. . . . The cake is not baked the same way each time. It must taste good at the end of the baking. That's where faith comes in. If you are not comfortable with the doctor you have selected, get another one!

Choosing a Doctor

When a parent makes the shift from his own home to yours, or to a nursing home near you, a first concern is to locate the right doctor. In areas where physicians are in short supply, you may have no choice; you may even have a problem finding a doctor or a group practice who will take new patients. Contact the nearest medical school, university teaching hospital, or medical center for names of doctors, stating the age and disability of your parent. You might also consult a floor nurse in a hospital or nursing home; or ask friends with elderly parents for suggestions.

If possible choose an older doctor, nearing the time of life himself when he may face geriatric problems. Older doctors are often more interested in those they treat than the treatments they select, more likely to see the whole person, and have a perspective on the ills of the aged person. Don't be afraid to ask questions. How does he feel about various treatments for the dying aged? Is he willing to investigate the basis for a patient's senility? Will he make visits to the nursing home you have selected? If he cannot be reached, who will take the calls? Will he answer specific questions you ask with specific answers? Is he short-tempered or patient with you? Developing communication with him at the beginning makes it easier to deal with him later in the event of your parent's stroke, heart attack, or senile dementia.

When a Parent Lives with You
In chapter 7, we dealt with some positive ideas for living together, should your solution be having your parent or parents live in your home. I cannot stress enough *beginning right* by firmly but lovingly explaining your family's routines. Unless your parent is senile, you must explain the general pattern of life: who works and when, what your children are allowed to do, mealtimes, rules for sharing bathrooms (if necessary); in short, include your parent in the existing pattern of your family's life. Some parents will go out of their way to accommodate you—praise them and thank them! Others will need to be guided and reminded until the pattern is established.

Sometimes a parent is well enough to assist by baby-sitting

and doing light housekeeping and cooking. This can help the families who have two working parents.

If your parent has been recently widowed, this traumatic change includes a grieving process. Remember, you cannot replace the husband or wife of your parent; neither can you make up for his or her home, friends, or activities. You can provide for comfort, but not for happiness! Insist on privacy for yourself and your spouse, whether or not hurt feelings follow.

Before you decide to have a parent live with you, think it through. Is it the only option financially? Does your spouse approve? Have you previously had a comfortable relationship with this parent? The health of all concerned must be considered, under today's intense stress.

The Nursing Home
As the ranks of the elderly increase, government, media, churches, and family have focused more on the quality of care in our nursing homes. Once considered a sort of "horror city" and last resort, many (though not all) have been upgraded to provide a competent level of care.

You may want to grade and assess the facilities available to you in the area where you and your parent live.

If your parent has little or no money, check the Department of Social Services (Welfare Department) and the Medicaid or Social Security offices. Some nursing homes are approved for both Medicare and Medicaid, some only for Medicare. Still others will not accept patients who must be admitted on Medicaid funds. Some offer skilled nursing care which means round-the-clock supervision for the severly disabled or ill. There are facilities which are private or denominational, requiring a down payment for long-term residency; others are public institutions. In looking at the nursing home option, consider three things:

finances, level of the parent's disability, future prognosis. A doctor should be involved in your decision. Investigate the nearest nursing homes which offer the care you need and can afford. Private nursing home care can be very expensive, though charges vary greatly.

Take a Positive Attitude

As you investigate and pray, ask God to confirm to you His best choice. Look for these 10 positive signs as you assess the facilities:

• The home is clean and neat without appearing sterile and cold.

• The staff is open and friendly, willing to spend time with you, give you a tour, and answer your questions in full.

• A general atmosphere of friendliness and caring prevails. Patients' rooms are decorated with mementos from home. Walls are not bare.

• The staff includes an adequate number of RNs, LPNs, aides, and orderlies.

• Supervised training is given to aides. Since they personally assist patients, this is an important consideration.

• The licensed dietician is able to provide special dietary requirements under a doctor's order.

• Licensed physical therapists are available.

• Patients are clean, hair combed, and those who are able are up in chairs or wheelchairs by late morning.

• Check bulletin boards, dayrooms, recreational facilities for programs. Ask if there is a director of activities.

• Most physicians and families of patients approve the facility.

If you have never visited a nursing home you may be depressed by patients in wheelchairs and using walkers. Some will be disoriented or withdrawn. If your parent is mentally alert and can hear well, ask if roommates are "paired": those able to relate to one another and enjoy company and activities should be, if possible, in the same room. Extremely ill or senile patients are better paired together. A caring staff will be trained to assess the needs and personalities of patients and attempt to do all they can to make a parent's living situation as pleasant as possible.

Perhaps your parent will spend only a few weeks in the nursing home, returning to his home or yours after a convalescence, but if long-term confinement occurs, you will be entering a new phase of life—one of mixed emotions, a variety of decisions, and wearisome visits. Your obedience to God's Word and the help of the Holy Spirit are vital to you, your parent, and other members of your family.

13
In Everything
Give Thanks

"Rejoice always, pray without ceasing, in everything give thanks, for this is God's will for you in Christ Jesus." 1 Thessalonians 5:16-18

"In everything give thanks?" Marian's hands were raised in a gesture of refusal. "No way can I be thankful for this mess we're in!" She went about her duties responsibly, but grimly, caring for a father who was selfish and demanding.

On the other hand, Diane smiled, praised and thanked the Lord loudly, sweetly telling others how easy it was to be "Mother's helper." At home alone, Diane wept in her pillow, beating her fists in frustration.

I don't think either of these responses is what God intended. None of us *feels* thankful all the time, nor can we be thankful *for* all circumstances, but we can be thankful *in* them. Neither is it right to sound good and be bitter inside.

Real thanks in all things includes recognizing God's sovereignty, His keeping power, the constant presence of the Spirit. Allowing Him to walk ahead of us, beginning each day by turning it over to Him and, yes, thanking Him daily and consciously, improves our relationship with Him.

Earlier I spoke of the tension of accommodation—the pull between generations and between siblings. Some will be better listeners, more understanding than others. The dark side of life's changes exposes threats, taunts, and reprisals; the light side reveals caring, compromise, and compassion. Sometimes the dark and the light are mixed, causing tension as we determine direction, decisions, and priorities.

Recognizing Losses

Both generations suffer losses that must be recognized and acknowledged. Parents, whether accommodating or recalcitrant, often must leave lifelong homes, apartments, prized furniture, cars, friends, churches. Sometimes it means giving over control of finances, schedules, and routines which have been parts of their lives for so long. Depending on the personality and the mental stability of the parent, this presents varying degrees of trauma.

If you are the caretaker, your lifestyle is also affected. Suddenly you have time-consuming tasks that must be integrated with jobs, home duties, and relationships with spouse or children (who are not always in tune with your new responsibility). At this point you must accept what has happened—you can't turn back. You too may lose freedoms and time, perhaps also space and money, in order to care for a parent.

Probably the most devastating loss for you and your parent is his loss of mental capacity. Speaking at the American Psychiatric Association's Council on Aging in Washington, D. C., Dr. Gene Cohen of the National Institute of Mental Health said,

"No one labeled as senile should be placed in a nursing home without a thorough examination by an internist or family practitioner, neurologist, and psychiatrist" (*AARP News Bulletin,* Dec. 1982, p. 3). Such an examination might uncover depression or other treatable conditions caused by vitamin B deficiency, poor medication, or hearing and eyesight problems. If your parent has Alzheimer's disease or other dementing illness that cannot be cured, you may write to Alzheimer's Disease and Related Disorders Association (ADRDA), 360 N. Michigan, Chicago, Il 60601. Local chapters are being formed to help families cope with the stress related to this problem.

Establishing Priorities

Getting emotionally caught up in the new process of role reversal can cause changes in you and your family that may not surface immediately. In the first stages of moving, while providing new accommodations for your parent (whether in your home or another), you are busy physically and mentally; you are discovering feelings from the past that must be dealt with; you may be enlisting the help of your spouse, children, brothers or sisters. As events quiet down, you may find that you haven't. Your mind stays active at night, you question choices, you overcompensate for your parent's loss by giving too much of your own time.

Subtle changes may then occur. Your husband or wife indicates displeasure, or reacts by withdrawal and silence. Other family members may disagree with the choices that were made. It is time, then, to set yourself apart and evaluate your priorities. Remember, all that appears urgent is not necessarily *important*. If your own life reflects a wholeness from having priorities in order, that wholeness will flow outward, causing others to be calm and purposeful.

How do we accomplish this? First, we must accept life as it is, not as we think it should be. Wishing it were otherwise is a negative use of energy. Being realistic enables us to list our priorities and goals so that we may integrate them into our lifestyles, as well as to take steps to correct those that are out of order. We must praise and thank God as we work on this. Pray without ceasing (keeping thoughts, needs, and thanks lifted to God). Listen for negative phrases: "I wish. . . ." "I don't like. . . ." "I can't even. . . ." It's impossible. . . ." Consciously practicing positive ways of speaking will help us as well as our listeners.

Understanding the Feelings of Others

Second, wholeness comes from recognizing the needs of others precious to us. By letting a mother know that we understand her feelings of loss, by praising her for every small acceptance of them, we encourage her to flow with the tide, rather than play tug-of-war with our emotions. She too, if able, needs to understand our priorities, so honesty is important. If we have a spouse and children at home, their needs must come first.

One conversation with my mother, while she was in the nursing home, shocked me at first, but opened the door for me to be honest with her. For some forgotten reason, I needed to skip some visits with her in order to be with my husband, a decision which I shared with my mother.

"I know," she lashed out. "Mothers don't count!"

I realized that, as the eldest of four, my mother had experienced a very close relationship with her own mother. In addition, she was past 30 when she married, and had always lived at home. I sat down near her. "Your mother always came first, didn't she?" I asked gently.

"Yes," answered this old lady, now in her late 80s.

"My husband must come first," I told her, and explained that this decision came from God's Word. "You know very well that I love you and care about you. That will always be true."

She calmed down. She did understand. Just as a child, she had felt a temporary disappointment and hurt. I left her room that day feeling whole, because I had not allowed an angry phrase to destroy communication or leave my mother in a state of rejection.

Recognizing the personhood of parents and of spouse and children is not the only route to wholeness. Loving and caring for ourselves, paying attention to our physical needs, our own activities, and rest requirements, enables us to be vital, growing persons.

"I had to give up my painting classes," sighed Elizabeth. "Mother expects to see me at the nursing home every day."

Elizabeth had assumed the role of martyr. After her mother died, Elizabeth lost interest in her hobby. She blamed her mother, nurtured an unforgiving heart, and became a disgruntled old lady herself.

Honest and creative thinking can help us continue our own lives in a healthy manner. When Bill and I made our decision to visit the Holy Land, I felt a real peace. Before I left, I made funeral plans for both parents. I selected caskets, talked with the funeral director, picked out clothes, and laid them aside. In the event of a death during our 10-day leave, the body would be held in a closed casket, and the funeral would take place on our return. Some might consider this callous; I believe it was being realistic.

Tough Love

You cannot change your parent's life situation, his state of health (except by good medical care), his age, or dependency.

If he blames you for any of these, refuse to carry this "baggage." Reject this load. By being reasonably attentive and caring, and doing what is necessary, you exhibit "tough love." Your parent is an imperfect human being, who may be carrying baggage from the past that *he* has never learned to lay down. Why perpetuate this situation by carrying a case full of resentment too? Sometimes it is only by looking back that we see ourselves as resentment carriers. We can be so busy acting out our grudges, nursing them, turning them over and over in our minds, allowing them to assail our health, that we are unaware of their devastating effects on us and those they are directed at. Break the chain of resentment and grudges by taking an honest look at them and asking God's forgiveness.

Unforgiveness *must* be dealt with. Recognizing that God forgives us when we ask Him is truly a reason for rejoicing; and should bring us to forgive our parents (whether they ask for it or not). The father who left home and rejected you, the mother who told you she never wanted you—yes, you must forgive them if you profess the name of Christ. You need also to share your most precious possession, the love of Jesus, if they do not know Him as Saviour.

My mother-in-law once told me that she was the last child, "an unwanted one." She spent her whole life trying to control people, take over situations, prove herself. She didn't know she was crying out, "See me! I am important!" No one had ever told her of her importance to God to free her from this shackle. When my father-in-law died in his 60s, my mother-in-law "expected" we would come to live with her in her big house. (I was then pregnant with my third child.) She was a healthy, vital person, but demanding. When my husband told her we would not move, she cried out, "What will people think of a son who doesn't want his mother?"

Will to Forgive

Parents can make us feel guilty, resentful, and unforgiving, but we must will to forgive them and not allow ourselves to be trampled or herded in unhealthy directions.

Later in life, my husband needed his mother's forgiveness for his attitude toward her. She didn't understand why he asked her for it, but she granted it. It was then that a full-blown physical healing occurred in Bill's life. Resentment and lack of forgiveness often block the healing Jesus longs to give.

Guilt complicates life by causing us to do too much or too little for a parent; to overcompensate for a parent's loss, or to avoid contact in order to (mistakenly) avoid the sense of guilt. Guilt may cause depression, physical ailments, and loss of energy, which in turn produce hostility as we drag ourselves through the days, trying to perform as good children should. As we feel hostility toward the parent, more guilt results. It is a merry-go-around we don't need to ride. As we *will* to forgive, God will give His grace.

After we lay down the baggage, we experience a freedom that carries us through those last years with a dependent or dying parent. The help of the body of Christ is very crucial for those experiencing these times. If a prayer group, Bible study fellowship, or prayer partner upholds us at this time, then all—parents, brothers, sisters, and their families—will feel the prayers of God's people.

How can the church community help during those days when death is close? In his pastoral letter (see chapter 11), Bishop Sullivan also wrote:

> We must commit ourselves to providing more attention to the pastoral care of the dying. . . . We must recognize and support the gift of those who are called to minister to the

dying, and we must recognize the need for training all ministers in how to deal with this important part of reality.

Also, the church must not neglect its obligation to prepare people for the moment of entrance into eternal life. There are currently movements which encourage greater consideration of the human and spiritual dimensions of death and dying; these should be encouraged, especially within the context of the life-affirming faith of the Christian. Efforts can and should be made to foster education, reflection, and prayer on the Christian concept of death. Ultimately, it is in the order of Christian faith, not physical reality, that death has lost its sting (see 1 Cor. 15:55-57).

The time of caring for parents is a difficult one, but it provides an opportunity to exercise our faith, stretch ourselves toward wholeness, become more loving and accepting of others. In turn, if we are not called home early, or if the Lord tarries, we too will take our places among the elderly.

As we seek to minister effectively to parents and families, it is well to emphasize a few simple truths to keep ourselves on course: First, spend time daily in prayer and in God's Word. Listen for the guidance of the Spirit. Second, remember that we can provide for our parents' comfort (and it is our duty to do so), but we cannot provide for their happiness. Third, what may seen urgent is not always important. Evaluate choices and decisions in light of this thought. Be positive in thoughts and action. Fourth, if we need help to free ourselves of unforgiveness, guilt or resentment, we must seek help from a pastor or other counselor, a trusted friend, or an adult child; get another's perspective on the problem.

Rejoice—for He is Lord! Pray without ceasing—He hears and answers! In everything give thanks for this is God's will in Christ Jesus.

Epilogue
The One Who Holds My Hand

"The steps of a man are established by the Lord; and He delights in his way. When he falls, he shall not be hurled headlong, because the Lord is the One who holds his hand. I have been young and now am old; yet I have not seen the righteous forsaken, or his descendants begging bread. All day long he is gracious and lends; and his descendants are a blessing." Psalm 37:23-26

"Every once in a while," Edith said, "I think, *Oh, I must remember to tell Mother that!* Isn't that crazy—she's been dead for two years!"

I have never done that. But those of us whose parents have died have some particular time or place that triggers a pang of remembrance. For me it's when I am selecting a greeting card. I see "To Mother and Dad at Easter," or "To Mother and Dad on Their Anniversary," or "Happy Valentine's Day to My Parents." The first time this occurred, I thought, *Never again will I be able to pick out a card for my mother and father.*

149

Soon after Mother's death, my husband looked at me strangely and said, "They're gone—your parents and mine. We're the older generation now."

Whether you are 35 or 55, you have probably given some thought—however fleeting—to a picture of yourself as a senior member of your family and community. The earlier you prepare yourself for this in a healthy and constructive manner, the more rewarding that time will be. Much has been said about "when are we old?" However we may reject it, 40 (certainly a prime time!) is considered the beginning of middle age; and if 55 sounds young and vigorous to you, remember that the American Association of Retired Persons recruits members of that age! *Over 65* is a phrase used for everything from discussion of retirement to TV commercials selling insurance. Your physiological age determines when you are a *senior citizen.*

Whatever our ages, the Lord is the One who holds our hands, and as we pray and seek to do His will, He motivates people and sets in motion help for His people of all generations.

Preparing for Old Age

What can we do now, to prepare ourselves for old age as a time of wisdom and fulfillment?

• Spend time with the Lord daily as a discipline and He will guide in plans and decisions.

• Review priorities and goals regularly. Make changes as life changes.

• Stay flexible. Sometimes do something we don't enjoy in order to stay flexible. Deliberately change our schedules and vary our routines often. No ruts allowed.

• Pursue hobbies we like.

• Practice good health rules in the areas of eating, exercise, and rest.

• Refrain from criticizing others, except in context of issues. Allow others freedom to be themselves in Christ.

• Maintain communication with family members, even when we disagree with their opinions or lifestyles. We must listen, be sensitive to their problems, and open to their suggestions. This builds the foundation for cooperation later in life, when we are the elderly parents.

• Practice compassion and kindness.

• Love ourselves in the sense of recognizing our worth in God's sight. Be aware of and do all we can to enhance the good in us.

• Write down the qualities we would like to have when we are old, and start now to implement them in our lives.

• Leave our houses in order for those who follow. Prepare now so that our loved ones will not be overwhelmed by our inadequate preparations for death.

As I write, I see the areas in my life that need improvement and renewal. I believe as we examine these suggestions, the Holy Spirit will show us individually where we are negligent, and where we can make changes that will give us peace as we age, and produce peace in others.

Unfortunately, it is usually true that the older we get, the less accommodating we become; yet there is greater need for us to be accommodating toward others—not becoming dolts or doormats, but understanding that each person has his own weaknesses and strengths, his own cares and priorities.

Our imperfections, our failures, our unforgiveness should lead us to seek the Perfect One, to forgive ourselves for failure and forgive others for theirs. The Perfect One is there all the time for the seeking; failure can be put behind us, spurring us on to inspired goals. Forgiveness is not only possible and desirable, it is mandatory if we are to live sanctified lives.

Even before my active commitment to Christ as Lord, and while I was producing and hosting a daily television show, I learned that failure must be put behind me. If a show went badly, or I sensed a poor performance, I said to myself, "It's over—there's nothing I can do about it now. Tomorrow I have another chance to do better." Doesn't that translate into our spiritual lives?

The excitement of knowing a faithful God through adversity makes each day worth living. It is matched only by the excitement of sharing the Lord with others—family members, friends, and the people who cross our paths in the course of daily life. Then we can say with Paul,

> I have fought long and hard for my Lord, and through it all I have kept true to Him. And now the time has come for me to stop fighting and rest. In heaven a crown is waiting for me which the Lord, the righteous Judge, will give me on that great day of His return. And not just to me, but to all those whose lives show that they are eagerly looking forward to His coming back again (2 Tim. 4:7-8, TLB).